Schooling Scotland

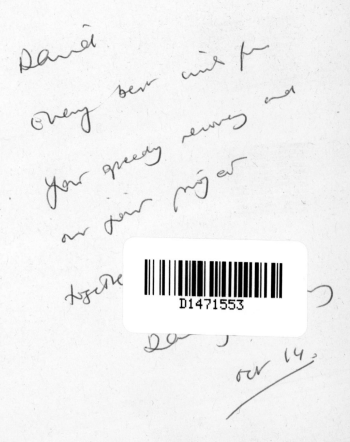

David

every best wish for
your speedy recovery and
our joint project

together

[signature]

oct 14

Schooling Scotland

Education, equity and community

Daniel Murphy

ARGYLL ✠ PUBLISHING

First published by Argyll Publishing in 2014.

Registered Office 1 Rutland Court, Edinburgh

© Daniel Murphy

The moral rights of the author have been asserted.

A catalogue record of this book is available from the British Library

ISBN 978-1-908931-61-0

*This book is dedicated to the
many colleagues, pupils and parents
from whom I have learned so much
over my forty one years in school education.*

Contents

Author's preface

The *Postcards from Scotland* series **is one of the exciting**
ways in which the civic community of Scotland has been
engaging in debate about Scotland's future, a future in which
school education will play a major role. I have tried to use
the experience and knowledge built up in my forty years in
school education to take general readers, as well as those
directly involved in schools, in behind some of the headline
issues and to convey the complexity and excitement of the
challenges facing our schooling system. There are many
things I think we can and should do to improve Scottish
schooling but there has been remarkable progress since I
started teaching in 1974. In my tour of some schools in
different parts of Scotland last year, it was delightful to meet
so many fine young people and their enthusiastic teachers.
My journal of that tour has been posted online on the home
page of the book at http://www.postcardsfromscotland.co.uk/
book_07.html. I encourage you to read it. It's an easy
narrative and gives a real insight into some of the people
behind the statistics, the people who make the generalisa-
tions of policy real. In school education, individual people
matter.

Also online at that link are further sources and references
to reports, research evidence and articles which support the

arguments of the book. Please browse through the evidence listed there and use the weblinks which can take you directly to many of the sources themselves. Included with the references are some detailed evidence summaries about key aspects of Scottish education which I prepared while researching for the book.

The last of the online resources supporting the book and available from the link above is a list of the abbreviations used in the book. In the text, full names are given along with the abbreviation only on the first occasion that an organisation is named.

This book is based on what I have learned during my career. I have learned from some things I did well, and some I did badly, from what I read and what I heard. I have learned from many of the people I worked alongside: from family and friends, from pupils and their parents, from colleagues in and out of schools. I want to thank especially those who made a special contribution to the learning I did while researching and writing this book: the staff and pupils and supportive local authorities of the schools which I visited for the online journal – thanks to Room 13 in Caol Primary School, Prestonpans Infant School, St John's Academy on Perth's North Inch Community Campus, Auchenharvie Academy, Bucksburn Academy, St Bernadette's Primary Larbert, Scottish Borders Council; thanks to colleagues who were willing to talk over some of the issues with me – Dan McGinty, Bob Currie, Danny McClure, Dave Johnstone, Ken Cunningham, Jim Fleming, Jackie Dunlop, Dee Torrance, Jacqueline Morley, the team at Talking Mats (Margo, Sally and Lois); thanks to my wife Joan, who was always willing to read, to challenge, to support, to discuss; thanks to Carol Craig whose direct and clear editorial feedback helped give shape to what was in danger of becoming too long and too formless a tour through every aspect of Scottish schooling. Some of the examples used in the book owe a debt to my earlier book, *Professional School Leadership: Dealing with Dilemmas*, Edinburgh: Dunedin Academic Press (2013 2nd edition) and I am grateful to Dunedin for permission to use these in an adapted form.

A brief note on terminology. The word 'pupil(s)' is used as the precise generic term for those enrolled in Scotland's educational institutions. Although for some it carries historic overtones of the regimented hierarchical character of some school communities of the past, none of these are intended here. It simply applies better across the whole age range than 'students' or 'young people'. The term 'student(s)' refers to someone enrolled in a course in further or higher education or to a mixture of school and FE/HE students. 'Child/children' is used as a general term for all school age children to avoid more clumsy frequent repetition of 'children and young people', but where all those referred to are older, the term 'young person/people' is used. Lastly, I have tried to avoid conflating 'schooling' with 'education'. 'Schooling' is what happens in, or is structured by, schools. Education is a much wider concept, involving learning within and outwith schools.

Lastly, as is customary, I can assure the reader that although many people have contributed to the arguments and evidence that follows, the mistakes and opinions are entirely my own. I welcome corrections and correspondence and encourage you to join in online debate and discussion on the topics raised. The book's homepage is http://www.

postcardsfromscotland.co.uk/book_07.html. There you will find a link to a facebook page and a twitter hashtag (#SchoolingScotland) for you to contribute to further discussion and debate, as well as my blog and twitter contact details if you want to follow up any issues with me directly.

Introduction

Many of the children born now will, if current trends in life expectancy continue, live through the rest of the 21st century. Our complicated post-industrial, rapidly changing society is insecure, faces unpredictable environmental changes, worries about the dominance of an all-consuming materialist culture and its impact on our well-being as well as the well-being of the planet we share[1]. The rationale of the *Postcards from Scotland* series states that 'it is becoming increasingly clear that Western societies will have to make huge changes. In short, we cannot go on in the same vein: we need to envision and enact a radically different future'. The books in the series aim 'to help develop new thinking in a readable and accessible format and to publicise, to a much greater audience, some of the projects in Scotland which are already aiming to help bring about a new way of living.'

Scottish schooling is certainly changing in response to these challenges, but is it changing enough? The millions who have watched Ken Robinson's hugely popular online TED talks on the lack of creativity in contemporary schooling or Sugata Mitra's talk about his 'hole in the wall' experiment and 'self organised learning environments' (if you haven't yet, you should) must wonder at how much of children's potential is unrealised in the tightly controlled systems of schooling. If visitors to the 'open learning' website can already access over a thousand courses from leading world universities free of charge, very soon we may ask, 'who needs school?'

I have an insider's knowledge and understanding of the Scottish school system, as a teacher, headteacher and tutor to trainee headteachers. In 2013, I enriched my own experience further by visiting some great schools in different parts of Scotland and have written up my experiences in an online journal.[2] It is intended to complement the book with an up-to-date, real life portrait of the variety and excitement of the work going on up and down the country. It gives a vivid inside view into how schools have changed and are changing for the better. My 'journal' of this tour illustrates some of the positive, inspiring work going on in our schools. In this book I draw on that 'tour', as well as forty years work across the Scottish schooling system and wide reading in school education internationally to answer two fundamental linked questions:

a) Can today's schooling system provide the best education for all children growing up in Scotland, now and in the future?

b) If not, what should be done to improve the schooling system?

In answering these questions, I conclude that Scottish schooling can do much better, but only if Scotland understands better the complexity of the social forces which operate within schools and renews its vision of what schooling is for and what it can do – a vision which recognises that schooling is only a part of education and that all of us in Scotland have a role to play – 'it takes all Scotland to raise a child'.

There is some great work going on in Scottish schools just now, as illustrated in my online journal. It is as good as the school experience of any children anywhere in the world. But there are also schools, teachers and pupils struggling to keep up. Public discussion about making sure all Scotland's children get the best education usually focusses narrowly on 'what can schools do better?', but schools work within a national framework, some aspects of which adversely affect some pupils, teachers and schools more than others. In outlining some of the challenges for the future, the book draws attention to an inequity in our current system which holds some children back, and argues for a stable long-term reconnection of schooling and community.

In the course of my argument I assume that current initiatives, such as developments in the teaching profession, remain in place, but I go further to outline a number of specific recommendations and draw them together in the short concluding chapter. I do not see these recommendations as an agenda for immediate change or for disruptive revolution in the system – but taken together, they amount to an evolutionary redesign of Scotland's schooling system to deliver better education, greater equity and stronger community. The discussion is aimed at *every* citizen of Scotland, not just those directly involved in schools (teachers, support workers, parents or pupils). Schooling, and the part it has to play in the education of our children, is everybody's affair. Although written before the imminent referendum, the arguments of the book apply equally in a devolved or independent Scotland. The book identifies eight important system issues to promote long-term positive change in our schooling system. These are written up in boxes as they occur in the text and summarised in the conclusion on pages 121–124.

CHAPTER ONE
Equity

Diversity

Let's imagine it's 18th September 2014, the day of our Scottish referendum and that you are standing with me in front of a comprehensive school house assembly, something I did often as headteacher of three Scottish comprehensive schools. Imagine that you're looking round the hall at the sea of faces. We can see Scotland's future right there, three or four hundred teenagers, a cross section of humanity. What a privilege to be here with them. So many different life stories, identities, motivations, yet here we share the same experience. In today's assembly, we'll explain the arrangements for voting in the school's 'mock referendum', in which everyone, not just those aged 16 and 17, will have a vote, then introduce some pupils to advertise a lunchtime fundraising sale, then the winner of 'This School's Got Talent', a third-year boy whose schoolwork is unremarkable, will take our breath away with a standout solo. We always try to share some successes each week, and there is usually a lot to share, but whatever the content of the assembly, just being physically together helps us understand better who we are, how 'we' become 'us' – more than a collection of disconnected individuals, but part of the big bustling varied community that is a comprehensive school. As you and I glance round the room, this is what the eyes of the headteacher, privileged to be a part of these lives, see:

There's a girl who is worried about exam results – will she get the five A passes she needs to apply to study medicine at university? Next to her is a boy whose preoccupation is working out how to speak to a girl he fancies. Many here haven't thought about school since the 4 pm bell yesterday. One helped his uncle in his plumbing business at the weekend and wishes he was still there. Some spent the weekend at Boys Brigade camp, some attended Mass, one played the organ at Methodist Church, four attended Islamic centre classes, some visited an ageing relative, some went with their dad and his dad to watch football in Glasgow. Some are on special diets, two with nut allergies, some vegetarians, some diabetic, some superfit, some superfat. Two proudly sport new tattoos, some fiddle with nose piercings, some have piercings that can't be seen. Twenty or thirty years ago, three children with Asperger's Syndrome would, along with another forty or more others with various learning difficulties or physical disabilities, have been in a separate school, but they are well kent here, among their peers, and we and they understand our humanity better as a result. Some drink alcohol regularly, a few drink recklessly; some smoke fags and some smoke weed: two or three do so regularly with their mothers' dealer boyfriends – and one of these regularly disrupts classes, a victim of drug-induced psychosis. A few are on a slippery slope with cocaine. Some breakfasted on crisps on their way to school; some had porridge, toast and orange juice. Some left home angry but arrived smiling with their pals. Some forgot their homework, one hasn't done it because they ended up sleeping at their dad's house and their school bag is at their mum's. Two girls spent the whole evening with their mother, herself a teacher in another school, revising a piece of work they want to get 'just right'. Some watch every episode of East Enders *and some none. Some went to Turkey for their Easter holiday, several have been to Australia and some have never been as far as Glasgow. Three newly arrived Latvians stick together; they speak little English. Some spend a lot of time in their bedrooms, online, unsupervised, perhaps at risk but more often just learning. Some would be happy to play football all day every day and others would do anything to avoid getting changed into sports gear. After years of domestic violence, two sisters are trying to hold their lives together, working through a programme with CEDAR (Children Experiencing Domestic Abuse Recovery) which includes rebuilding their relationship with their abused mother. Another two sisters have come to school together planning how they will surprise their mother for her 40th birthday. Some are on to their third Ipad, some have no broadband at home. All live in houses with running hot and cold water but two are in a house where there was no money to feed the meter this morning – in fact there is often only cold water – while four live in homeless hostel accommodation. One girl had a letter about the humanitarian consequences of the Syrian conflict published in* The Observer *at the weekend, a group of boys are making money from their own commercial gaming website, but some sitting in the same hall can barely read at all. Some will forever believe they are 'no good at maths'. Five have parents who are solicitors, four have parents who are refuse collectors, one has a parent who is an MSP, thirty five have parents who work in shops, many have parents whose jobs lack security, a few have relatives in the forces, and some don't know their parents at all. One girl is sitting worrying whether she should ask the teacher she confides in about the 'morning after pill'. There are two in care whose father is in Carstairs for life on account of murdering their mother a few years back. There are many more whose fathers cook at the weekends. Almost no-one ate' 'five a day' yesterday and half a dozen have had no fruit or veg in the past week. Two children in wheelchairs will be the first to scoot out of assembly and make their way to the lifts. One, with athetoid cerebral palsy, uses a hand switch to operate his chair and a different switch for the communication device he uses to speak and which goes everywhere with him. He often brings a smile to our faces with his pre-programmed jokes ...*

I could carry on – there is no easy place to stop exploring the diversity, the individuality of the little mini-communities of our comprehensive schools. In smaller, more intimate early years or nursery settings, or in community-based primary schools, the school may be less diverse, and the worries and the issues different, but the possibilities, the variety of talents and enthusiasms, all the diversity of the adult community around is found in microcosm in the pupils of the inclusive school. Our complex plural democracy values this diversity and the individuality that goes along with it. Through the social experience of the comprehensive school, Scotland's future citizens better understand our plural society and the different paths to adult life that are open to them – or closed to them, for they do not all have equal chances, nor do they all put in equal effort.

Inequalities

Some of these 'inequalities' are seldom debated and are accepted as part of the natural diversity of any human population – good looks, sporting ability, musical talent. In the past thirty years, many of the previous gender inequalities of access and performance have been eroded. National statistics are regularly monitored for possible inequalities related to gender, ethnicity and a variety of other categories and a variety of legislative requirements and policy advice address equality of opportunity.

An important inequality that never features in national debate is age: the youngest Scottish children start school at four and a half, much earlier than most European equivalents and six months younger than their English counterparts at every stage of schooling. There is no defence for this position educationally and several arguments against it. Younger pupils, often the poorest wee souls in Primary 1, on average do less well than older ones within the same year all the way through school up to and including performance in national examinations at age 15/16. In a final unfair throw of the dice, those born after September in a given intake year, and who wish to leave school to seek employment at the end of S4, have to stay on an extra half year till Christmas of S5. In many schools, it is inefficient to provide a special August to December curriculum for the 'Christmas leavers', so, after eleven years when they never quite catch up with their older peers, they experience a poorer curriculum in their final, additional, half year.

Issue #1: Scotland should immediately raise the school starting date to a standard five years at 15th August and abolish the 'two stage' leaving date, an historical anomaly in the system which, at the start and end of their school careers, can badly affect some pupils caught in the age trap. This would ensure that larger numbers of children are better prepared for schooling, and this change alone, of the many open to the government, could enhance the educational experience of the largest number of pupils.

In contrast, the inequalities that result from poverty receive the most attention in political debate. They are starkly illustrated in the story of two typical Scottish boys which follows.

In August 2009, Jim and Ian, born within minutes of each other on 11th September 1997, the day of the last Scottish referendum, started secondary school together but only one of them, Jim, is still sitting in the assembly we just visited. Jim was born into a family in the most affluent 'decile' of the Scottish population (each decile is 10 per cent or roughly half a million people) – among the richest and most favoured people on the planet. Ian was born into a family whose income is in the least affluent 'decile' of the Scottish population. These boys are now 17. They have unique personalities and abilities but in their health and educational development they match the 'average' for their decile and that means they have had very different schooling experiences.

Jim is now starting his sixth year and already has five 'Highers'. Through his school career, his parents paid for his music lessons, his expensive sports gear, tennis club membership, ski trips – a wide range of school-based learning activities beyond the classroom. While he will spend the next few years at university, he has no particular job in mind. Through family contacts and his degree-educated parents' knowledge of professional employment, he has ready access to specific advice and support in reviewing his many options. Scotland will spend more on Jim's education than on Ian's – six years of free schooling and a degree course heavily subsidised through general taxation. This extra investment will give him access to more secure employment, through which he can expect to earn substantially more than a non-graduate, but also to pay more tax.

Ian gained four Standard Grade awards at Level 3 (Foundation) and two at Level 4 (General). He felt little motivation to try hard at secondary school, since even when he tried, he 'wasn't very bright' (his own words). He left school as soon as he could. Before he left, he received specific career advice, but he and his family have no overview of the complex potential pathways into employment or training which make up Scotland's messy post-16 offer to those not in school. He had an interview arranged for a construction skills programme at the local college, but on the morning of the interview, his route to college was blocked by members of a gang from a neighbouring area and he had to escape quickly. Afraid of meeting them again, he did not turn up for the interview and lost interest in the college option. Ian's mother works alongside the wife of a local painter – this led to occasional cash-in-hand casual painting work. Ian is as likely to get longer-term work through contacts like this within his known and trusted community as he is through formal schemes. Insecure work on the fringe of the economy is a likely job future for Ian, a career as one of capitalism's necessary supply of flexible labour.

At infancy, Jim had a healthier birthweight. At age three he was using language more fluently. He is also likely to live ten years longer than Ian and experience less ill health during this longer life. Jim is less likely to smoke or have alcohol-related health problems or experience mental health problems such as depression. These statistics predict that Ian is likely to get a worse deal right throughout his life. If we compare him with his great-grandparents or some contemporaries in other parts of the world, in Syria or South Sudan for example, his life expectancy, health and education look better. But this is Scotland not Syria. Today, not the 1930s. Our devolved government has had control over education and health since 1998. What did Jim do to deserve his better chance, or Ian his worse chance? I have chosen Jim and Ian, and not their sisters Catherine and Elaine, since one of the success stories of recent years has been the inverting of the gender imbalance, at least in schools. Over my lifetime, given equal opportunities, girls have overtaken and now persistently outperform boys in school-level attainment. But relative affluence is a good predictor of school attainment for both boys and girls. Although both Catherine and Elaine are likely to outperform their brothers in school attainment, the gap between the two girls is the same.

Schools are at the heart of this inequality in contemporary life. Different outcomes from school lead to different possible destinations in life. These inequalities are nothing new. In 1973 as I completed my first university degree, swithering over my future, I read a small book called *Born To Fail* (1973) which suggested that almost twenty per cent of Scottish children were 'born to fail' and concluded that 'education as a "social distributor" of life chances often compounds rather than eases the difficulties of disadvantaged children.'[3] I entered teaching, at least in part, to try to change that, to even out the playing field in Scotland. In my forty years in Scottish schools, I have worked in the most and the least affluent parts of Scotland, with some of the most difficult-to-reach young people, excluded long-term from mainstream schools, and with many who loved school. In every setting, I met many real-life Jims and Ians, Catherines and Elaines. While I'd like to think that I, and teachers like me, made a difference to individual young people, the OECD report of 2007 made clear that structural problems of inequality remain as obdurate as ever:

> Scotland's high overall achievements in mathematics, reading and science, and the comparatively small proportion of low achievers in these learning domains bears out the strengths of ... a widely accessible and high quality system of secondary schools ... [But] who you are matters a great deal more in Scotland than what school you attend, and 'who you are' is defined largely in terms of socio-economic status. [4]

In 2013, the National Children's Bureau published an update on *Born To Fail*, called *Greater Expectations*, with depressingly familiar statistics for the UK, echoed in a recent Joseph Rowntree report into poverty and schooling in Scotland. Table 1 below, linking relative affluence and school attainment, shows the character of this 'inequality' very clearly.[5] It relates the tariff score of pupils to their level of relative affluence. Each pupil's tariff score is calculated by adding up 'points' awarded for different school qualifications – passes at Advanced Higher are worth more points than Higher, an 'A' pass gets more than a 'B' and so on. The 'least affluent' 20 per cent (the bottom two Scottish Index of Multiple Deprivation (**SIMD**) 'deciles' – each decile is 10% of the population) attain only around half the 'tariff score' of the 'most affluent' 20 per cent. Although the tariff scores of the least affluent have increased by around sixty points in recent years, so have all the others. All are improving so the gap stays the same.

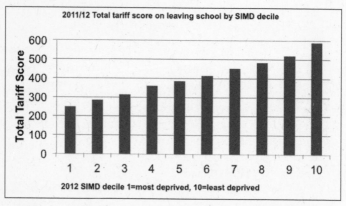

Table 1: Tariff score on leaving school by SIMD decile.

SIMD also predicts job success. The more affluent your parents, the more likely you are, like Jim, to get the 'top jobs'[6] or to go into a 'positive destination (a job, course in college or university or training place) on leaving school.[7] Specific targeted programmes by schools, colleges, Skills Development Scotland (**SDS**), local employers and voluntary agencies have reduced the proportion of school leavers who are 'NEET' (not in employment, education or training) in recent years but the figure is still unacceptable. Almost fifty per cent of those whose highest level of school attainment is Standard Grade Foundation Level end up 'NEET'. A generation or two ago, youngsters like Ian might have gone straight into a factory or mining job, learning about life while earning within a well-established work culture. In the more complicated, fragmented post-industrial economy, Ian's current experience is not untypical. Poor school attainment makes low-skilled insecure entry into the job market much more likely. It's not only outcomes that are unequal – we never even bother to calculate how much less the country spends on Ian's education compared to Jim's.

There are Ians in every part of Scotland. In rural areas, this may not show up at all in the datazone statistics – the numbers involved are small and balanced out by nearby affluence. However the densest concentrations are in west central Scotland, in the City of Glasgow in particular. The first industrial revolution scarred the community life of many in the growing Glasgow conurbation. The end of that industrial period was equally traumatic, throwing men out of work, disrupting the relationships and social vision that had been built around the hard industrial culture of factory, shipyard and mine. The average tariff score of pupils leaving Glasgow's schools directly reflects Glasgow's high levels of relative poverty. West central Scotland's industrial history makes Scotland a very different society from the Scandinavian countries which some want Scotland to copy. They had a more evolutionary, less disrupted, journey from their stable peasant past into the 21st century.

Many teachers and many schools in Scotland are making a difference to the lives of their pupils right now. The levels of attainment of Scottish school leavers in every 'decile', including those of the lowest attaining pupils, have risen consistently over the past thirty years. Commentators, such as the authors of the Rowntree report 'Closing the Gap' (2014) and the Scottish Labour Party's 'Mind the Gap' (2014), have summarised the ways in which schools and the schooling system are presently working to reduce inequalities. Many of the teachers working in the least affluent parts of Scotland are among the most dedicated and hardworking people I know, teachers who would walk every extra mile for their pupils, and who chose to work in exactly those schools because they believed they could make the most difference there. Colleagues from Glasgow I have worked alongside would shine in any school anywhere in the world. National and local government, through the policies highlighted in the next chapter, and through short-term initiatives such as 'New Community Schools' have shown commitment to reducing educational inequality. Every teacher can tell inspiring stories of individual children from the least affluent backgrounds who have achieved the highest standards, but the statistics of Table 1 above tell us that these are still exceptions: despite all the good work to improve the chances of less affluent kids it remains the case that the more affluent you are, the more you benefit from school education. It is easy to see why.

The very things that improve the chances of the very poorest – individual support, continuing professional development for teachers, a warm and supportive ethos, high expectations – also improve the learning of all other pupils. In a competitive system, when those at the bottom of the ladder improve, those above them may work harder to maintain their advantage. Even if every pupil in Scotland attained five Highers in their school examinations, do we imagine that the children of doctors, lawyers and bankers would then take up equal numbers of low-paid insecure service sector jobs? Is it not likely that the threshold for entry to desirable university courses in medicine and law would increase to five Advanced Highers, that richer parents would pay for more tutoring, more internship experience? The competitive credential inflation of recent years, including unpaid internships and expensive privately-funded Masters degrees, has only increased, rather than decreased, the potential advantages of those who are already advantaged.[8]

The 'elephant in the room' is our unequal society. Time and again, in a variety of studies in different countries, the inequality of wider society is seen to lead to the inequality of schooling, not the other way round. Cristina Ianelli's review of the evidence on social mobility in Scotland concludes, for example, that 'educational policies on their own are not powerful enough to change patterns of social mobility which are mainly driven by labour market and social class structures'.[9] The recent research survey by Hoskins and Barker concluded that patterns of relative social mobility have remained stable in the UK at least since the 1930s, in line with most other European countries – those privileged by wealth, powerful social networks and inside knowledge of high status occupations continue to use their position and resources to advantage their children.[10] What Halsey pointed out in 1977 remains true today: '. . . middle class families have always adapted to the current institutional regime in ways designed to maximise their chances of securing favourable opportunities for their offspring . . .'[11] As many radical commentators have argued, schooling tends to replicate rather than reduce the inequalities of society.

What, then, is the way forward? To start with, we need to be clearer in our thinking about 'equality'. In mathematics, equality is absolute – quantities, numbers, statistics are either equal or they are not. But in democratic social life, equality is more complicated. Different values lead to different choices and consequent diversity.

Firstly, not everyone chooses those options that lead to more money or status, or wants equality of income. Numbers cannot measure everything that we value: 'happiness', for example. Perhaps Ian is a great support to his mum, happy in his friendships and in a great relationship with a steady girlfriend. Perhaps Jim is an unpleasant teenage presence around the house, miserable because he seems unattractive to girls. Many of the 'Ians' I taught in my career had a pleasant manner and a sparky intelligence, well attuned to their environment. Some of the 'Jims' were self-absorbed and arrogant. Maybe Jim and Catherine will choose to work in England or New York after graduation. Maybe Ian and Elaine are happy to live round the corner from their mums and bring up their children in a close extended family. Who is to say which is a better life? Socio-economic status and educational attainment statistics tell us nothing about some of the most important things in Jim's or Ian's lives. Whatever the statistics say, both have lives of equal value, lived in different ways. But the relationship between the income gap, the education gap and the health gap is inescapable and calls on our society to do more.

Second, social equality sits on a spectrum, not an exact point. The weakest form is equality of opportunity – it gives individuals the same choices, but takes no account of their different levels of advantage and handicap. The strongest form is equality of outcome – but in any democratic society diversity of outcome, and consequent inequality, is a necessary result of the freedom people value – a freedom that allows even those whose choices are limited to make different choices on how they spend their money and their time. The challenge is not to eliminate diversity and make everyone 'equal' but to find the correct balance point between the two great democratic ideals of freedom and equality – this is explored further in Chapter Three. Greater freedom for individuals increases inequality, whereas greater equality can only be brought about by social controls and restraints. The concept of 'equity', related to but different from equality, defines the balance point between freedom and equality.

Equity

Equity is not about precise statistics but about our sense of 'fairness', expressed through political process. Different societies and governments define equity differently. In the United States, the 'land of the free', greater freedom runs alongside greater inequalities. In Scandinavia, there is a different balance point, with higher levels of taxation delivering a welfare entitlement for all citizens: freedom (to spend money you have earned) is reduced by taxation, in the interests of greater social equality. For me, the balance point is quite clear – *disempowering* inequality of the kind which affected Ian's life, is unfair. Above a certain threshold, however, inequality matters less.

Wilkinson and Pickett's book *The Spirit Level* (2009) demonstrated that after this threshold level of income is reached, 'additional income buys less and less wellbeing.'[12] In the USA context, Nobel Laureate Daniel Kahneman's Gallup study of the relationship of income to well-being also identifies this effect: 'more money does not necessarily buy more happiness, but less money is associated with emotional pain.'[13] Michael Marmot's studies of social class and health, echoed in Scotland by Harry Burns, make clear that the 'threshold' is defined by a person's sense of autonomy – being in control of one's life, being able to make choices.[14] This requires an income above poverty. When people experience poverty, every choice is a reaction, not a plan; getting to the end of the week has enough challenges; choices are heavily restricted. Beyond a minimum 'threshold' level, income is no longer a disempowering factor.

Education, as well as income, can contribute to a sense of autonomy. Its 'currency' is not money but knowledge and learning skills; its 'capital' is not savings and investments, but an understanding of the complex interaction of credentials, jobs and professions and the educational pathways which lead to them and a sense of purpose and meaning in life. A key goal of the new Scottish curriculum is that pupils become autonomous self-motivated learners, but all teachers know that pupils vary greatly in their motivation and consequent effort. The current schooling system tends to reinforce these effects and teachers have to fight against them. At each stage of school, Jim became 'richer' in learning skills and consequently learning was more purposeful, difficult learning more achievable. From the earliest years of school, Jim's family had used their informed understanding of economy and society to help chart a pathway which led to desirable qualifications and beyond: one which Jim internalised in his thinking about the relationship between his schooling and his future life. In a self-reinforcing cycle of long-term commitment and short-term improvements in skills and knowledge, Jim became more motivated to learn and to work harder than Ian. Ian, comparing himself to Jim, became less motivated, just as any of us would if we were constantly forced into a competitive task with people who always do better than us.

Many reports (co-incidentally including one published on the day I finished writing this text) describe in detail the devastating effects of poverty on Scottish children.[15] International reports on progress towards the United Nations' commitment to 'Education for All' demonstrate the strong link between improvements in the income and education of mothers and consequent improvements in the life chances of their children.[16] We often think of this as an issue for poor countries, somewhere else, not for a rich developed country like Scotland. However, the argument developed throughout this book is that 'it takes *all* Scotland to raise a child' – that all of us in civic Scotland share in that responsibility. If Scotland wants Scotland's children to have a better start in life, there is nothing we can do that would have a greater effect than to *ensure that poor families have sufficient money*, that they are above Wilkinson and Pickett's 'threshold', where choices are easier, where it is possible to live more autonomous, less reactive, lives. Increasing the income of poor families may well be a much more effective educational intervention than any of the work done by teachers or in schools. How this should be done is a job for politicians – *that* it should be done should be a demand from all of us in a civilised society, committed to equity in our democratic life together.

Equity across school communities

School communities vary greatly in character. In many rural communities, where there is no local alternative, everyone sends their children to the local schools, save perhaps the lairds and a few others who may use residential private schools. In local 'omnibus schools' (schools for everyone – the original comprehensive schools), children from all social backgrounds mix together and learn with and from each other, but they are in a minority in Scotland. Private schools, particularly in the cities and above all in Edinburgh, educate a disproportionate number of the most affluent and only a very, very few of the least affluent. The economic changes of industrialisation and social rehousing led to socially uniform, but geographically separate, school communities in working class mining villages, industrial towns, council housing estates and middle class suburbs. This social segmentation in schooling is increased by the effects of parental choice. In the state sector, over 20 per cent of parents of primary age children and a slightly smaller number in secondary regularly choose a school other than the local school for their children, while around 20 per cent of parents choose a faith-based school, 99 per cent of which are Catholic.

The OECD statistical analysis of Scottish schools suggested that whether in a leafy suburb or a deprived housing area, the school makes relatively little difference to a pupil's potential success in examinations, when compared to the effect of the relative affluence or poverty of the home.[17] Nonetheless the *social* character of these schools differs markedly, with consequent differences in the educational experiences of their pupils. There are positives in choice and diversity. Where parents have made a positive choice to send their children to a school, whatever the reason – faith, attainment, social exclusivity, personal problems – the school can assume a greater degree of commitment. The strong bonds of faith schools, forged around shared values, is one of their most important qualities – values matter in education. Sometimes problems between individuals, between families, or within communities, can damage children and a 'change of scene' can be good for all concerned. Private schools, with their considerable private assets and independence, also show how schools can be run differently. They have much cleaner lines of accountability and are more flexible in their curriculum and staff management. In partnership with their parents and their motivated pupils, and with far greater resources at their disposal, they provide a good educational experience for some.

However, diversity can reduce equity if it becomes exclusive, building harmful barriers between individuals and communities. Private schools often use their independence to exclude those who do not fit in, financially and/or academically. Schools with a small proportion of children in the least affluent deciles carry a much lighter social burden, and consequent fewer social commitments than those with a high proportion of such children. There is much for teachers and local authorities to learn from the London Challenge[18], where, rather than competing with each other for pupils, schools and teachers shared problems and resources and worked together in a supportive network, accepting joint responsibility for all pupils in all schools in the network, rather than seeing other schools as potential competitors, or their pupils as someone else's responsibility. Where there is little internal diversity within a school, private or public, children lack valuable face-to-face experience of the challenges facing other young people and are distanced from the diverse society of which they are interdependent citizens. Successful pupils may, for example, come to see their achievements as entirely a result of their own efforts rather than, in some measure, a consequence of their social advantages.

In a mature system of school education, the strengths of diversity, private and public, should be brought together to benefit all children. Here are some starters for discussion: mid-career staff exchanges of teachers (all of whom were trained and educated at public expense); shared pupil participation in classes and in local civic enterprises; shared sporting facilities; shared community service; shared resources; a shared campus; shared Duke of Edinburgh, Cadet Force and outdoor pursuits. Private and public sector pupils and teachers can enrich each other's learning. Rather than enforcing a standard model, let private schools be required, as part of their charitable commitment, to negotiate and take ownership of their own 'public contribution' through collaborative agreements with other local schools for the benefit of all local children.

> **Issue #2:** Schools should work in partnership, in networks of neighbouring school communities, including private schools, to share responsibilities and increase opportunities for children from diverse backgrounds to work and learn with and from others. (see also issue#7)

Early years

The greatest flexibility and innovation lies in this expanding sector, which is not strictly a 'school' sector at all and hence is only briefly discussed here. There is a strong consensus across the political spectrum that spending more money on early years education would be worthwhile – whether universal provision or intervention targeted at specific social groups and designed to 'even up' a playing field which is already tilted against children from less affluent backgrounds before they start school. There is a vision, untested at a national level, that this will address educational inequality by getting to its roots. Developing trusting respectful relationships with the parents, based around a passionate commitment to the children, is the most important part of any successful work in this evolving field, yet many 'early years intervention' programmes seem to be based on the proposition that, if the home learning environment is comparatively poor, the best thing to do is remove the child from it for longer, as if it was possible to 'inject' the children with what they are missing at home. If the relationships are not right, this approach may simply set up an alienating gap between home and school, public service and the parent. From the beginning, the parent must be 'inside the tent', building a trusting partnership between state and home which can last through to age 18.

At 'Wee Pans', in my school tour, I saw mothers and fathers going into school from the earliest stages, effective programmes of study support to young mothers and no walls between school and community. Some of what is happening there costs money, but some of it is about opening up the right doors, making the right connections, putting people, parents, professional services, third sector organisations, in touch with each other, with the school as a community hub. While there is a lot of this kind of practice in early years, showing a new way for school and community to work together, the aims, standards, management and governance of early years provision – whether private or public – vary greatly. The extension of 'early years' provision to the calendar age of five which I have proposed will give some children the longer time they need to get ready for primary schooling and can only be beneficial.

Here as in other areas, the right balance is required. The least affluent have the least resources, the least power, the most difficulty with the formal systems of a society that they can easily feel are disempowering. 'The Growing Up in Scotland' (**GUS**) reports suggest that the least affluent households are less likely to use universal services than more affluent households, just as, at the opposite end of the education spectrum in higher education, the most affluent students benefit most from free tuition.[19] If not carefully managed, early years investment may, as in other schooling sectors, increase inequalities rather than reduce them. There are great possibilities, but it is too early to say if expansion will lead to hoped-for improvements or further reinforce exclusion and inequality. Targeted independent evaluation will be needed to ensure that interventions do not simply replicate the tilted playing field at a younger age.

* * *

In conclusion, this chapter demonstrates that current inequity challenges Scotland to be fairer to its poorest children, and to the youngest children in a given year group. No matter how hard individual teachers and schools work at it, they cannot make Scotland more equal. Schools are generally more equitable places than adult society, but the inequity of our wider society is built into the system, in secondary schools in particular. These themes of equity and equality run through the book and through the debates it encourages.

CHAPTER TWO
School education today

Almost everyone is, to some extent, an expert on schooling – an expert in his or her own experience – but individual experience is no guide to the variety of the bigger picture. At the macro-level of national policy, unlike in England where there has been constant system change over thirty years, the Scottish schooling system of neighbourhood primary and comprehensive secondary schools, run by multi-purpose local authorities, has remained largely intact. But there has been much change within that stable structure. To some extent both primary and secondary schools are still working through the implications of changes that started in 1965, when the Primary Memorandum advised that primary schools should adopt a 'child-centred approach', secondary school selection was abolished and comprehensive schools introduced. Along the way, there have been many ups and downs and a whirlwind of policies and guidance, but four complementary policies, centred on the individual child, begun under Labour and Liberal Democrat administrations and carried on by the SNP, summarise how Scottish schooling now puts into practice the values of those 1965 reforms: a school education appropriate for every child (not a select minority), social inclusion and support targeted where needed.

Four key policies

The Additional Support for Learning Act of 2004 (amended 2009) (**ASL**) and Getting It Right For Every Child (**GIRFEC**) are about *inclusion* and *support*. They share a belief that every child has unique learning needs and social experiences. For most children, most of the time, family life and the group learning of the mainstream classroom provide sufficient support for their learning and development, but some require specialist assessment and 'additional support'.

ASL replaces the older concept of 'special education', since *any* child may encounter barriers to learning – temporary or permanent; physical, cognitive, emotional, or all three – which may show up in learning, in relationships or in particular developmental difficulties. ASL requires local authorities to identify the barriers and agree, with the child, parents or carers, teachers, and other specialist services, what additional support is required. It presumes that all children, other than in the 'exceptional' circumstances allowed in the Standards in Scotland's Schools (2000) Act, should be educated in a 'mainstream school'.

GIRFEC looks at the whole child – at home, in school, in the community. It defines eight entitlements for all children growing up in Scotland using the acronym SHANARRI – all should be **S**afe, **H**ealthy, **A**chieving, **N**urtured, **A**ctive, **R**espected, **R**esponsible and **I**ncluded. Any problems should lead to targeted intervention and support, involving the child, parents and the appropriate agencies (social work, health, school etc.) working together for the benefit of the child. GIRFEC confirms that schools have a social as well as an educational role.

Curriculum for Excellence (**CforEx**) details the learning 'experiences' which every Scottish child should have and what they should be able to do as a result of their learning (the 'outcomes'). Like ASL and GIRFEC, it applies to every child, whatever barriers inhibit their learning

The Standards in Scotland's Schools (2000) Act (**SSS**) is about *quality*. It requires headteachers to prepare a development plan (now universally called a 'School Improvement Plan') in consultation with parents, pupils and staff and to publish an annual report on improvement. Local authorities have to ensure quality, taking action where necessary.

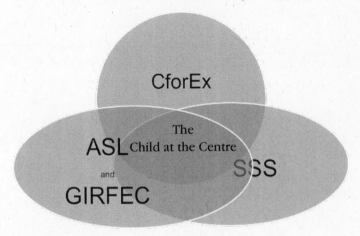

On paper, the policies work well but when the paper meets the people, life gets more complicated.

ASL and GIRFEC reviewed

Every state school in Scotland now aims to be an 'inclusive' school, able to respond appropriately to every child's needs.

The values of inclusion and individual support are as important as what these policies say. Relationships between teachers and pupils are better than they have ever been, many fewer children are now excluded from school for disciplinary reasons, while across Scotland, 'soft starts', 'nurture groups' and supportive programmes such as 'Seasons for Growth' provide a gentler, caring space for some vulnerable pupils. [20] Where this works well, as in the schools I visited on my tour, it's uplifting. A recent Scottish Government report shows progress but this is still uneven. A report by the Scottish Disability Equality Forum highlighted ongoing difficulties with access for those with physical disabilities, problems mirrored in another recent report into the education of the deaf.

There are many positive examples of inclusion, but also less successful examples. While pupils with additional needs are formally included when they attend a mainstream school, they can feel excluded through poor peer relationships, inappropriate educational programmes or teachers who lack specific knowledge or training. Parents may get into dispute with their local authority when they believe the local mainstream school cannot meet their child's unique needs and that specialist schooling would be better. Where a child's additional support needs concern their behaviour, in or out of school, issues of inclusion and exclusion play out in more difficult ways. The examples below illustrate these tensions. Underneath there is the question of budgets. Improved assessment and increased awareness have seen the number of pupils with identified needs increase significantly. Additional support costs money and local authorities have to balance the books. This is a decision for all of us. How much is Scotland willing to pay for all children to be fully included?

The complexity of inclusion

Example 1

Zander, a S3 boy aged 15, was excluded from school after repeated escalating incidents of aggressive threatening behaviour towards teachers. In accordance with the policy of inclusion, the best place for Zander to be educated is in his local school, so he is brought back into school but is 'supported' in potential flashpoint classes by a school learning assistant, Maya. Outside of school, Zander is a leading figure in the local gang culture. He is very popular with some of his peers and has a number of girlfriends. In school, he has low status academically. His resentment at this underpins a latent hostility to the teachers, which is in some cases reciprocated. In class Maya mediates the demands of the teachers. Without her there, sparks will fly. In the same class is Zak. Zak is on the child protection register. He is obviously neglected – smelly, unwashed body, unwashed clothes. Zak has an odd appearance and hangs out on his own at interval and lunchtime. Zak appears deeply miserable but does not cause trouble in class or disrupt lessons. Both need support to be 'included', but some teachers are angry that it is Zander who gets the extra resource of Maya's time when Zak 'deserves it more'.

Example 2

Two children with athetoid cerebral palsy, Esther and Fergus, attend neighbouring schools in the same town. Esther's parents are very happy for her to attend her local school, where she has made friends with some of the other pupils and is making progress in her learning, using a communication aid with a digital voice with the rest of the class and her teachers. Fergus' parents are not happy. They want him to attend a special school (run by an educational charity). They believe that this may give him a chance of being able to walk. They mistrust the local authority which they believe is acting solely on the basis of saving money (the cost of fees and of transport for the special school is approximately four times the cost of educating Fergus in his local school). The breakdown of trust has caused an unpleasant atmosphere between school and parents. Parents feel the school is hostile and defensive. Teachers feel that whatever they do for Fergus will never be enough.

GIRFEC has closed many loopholes in the state's role in looking after children e.g. some of Scotland's most vulnerable children are those 'looked after', both in care and also at home. Under GIRFEC, local authorities are required to offer support through into adulthood at age 25. The national GIRFEC website gives some excellent case studies of GIRFEC making a real difference to children's lives. But GIRFEC is also complicated. Some have argued that the 'therapeutic' approach is a method of 'producer capture' by which professionals 'persuade' 'clients' that they need 'support', encouraging dependence rather than resilience. If relationships between the professionals and the family are not good, GIRFEC can become a confusing, impersonal process and those most in need of support can be intimidated, angry, or just confused. I have sat in on meetings where one child and his mother were overwhelmed by all the different professionals working with the child (psychologist, teacher, speech and language therapist, social worker, adolescent mental health worker) and frequent staffing changes. For them, support was unwelcome intrusion. Defining problems as individual to the child may also address the wrong problem. The reason a child may be getting into difficulty often has as much to do with the community as with the child and the solution may lie in the community as much as the individual.

The collaborative working across public services that GIRFEC demands is not straightforward. Police, health, education and social work can work well together in short-term task groups but long term, collaborative working, even within GIRFEC, is made more difficult by differences in the systems – reports, budgets, management arrangements, rules of confidentiality, assessment criteria, paperwork. Some agencies follow a medical model – 'diagnose, treat, discharge' – which is quite different to how schools work. Some involved in a case may seem to be spending more time meeting than doing - writing up referral forms, assessment criteria, reports, case conference minutes. There can be tensions around resourcing – who pays for what? Such problems can also beset ASL meetings, when 'multi-agency assessments' are needed in order to create a co-ordinated educational plan for a child. Breakdowns in communication and joint working are often, in my experience, the result of the very complexity of the processes exemplified below.

The different expertise and knowledge of different professions are an important resource – specialist expertise needs protection and support, especially in a multi-disciplinary team, but there is always work to be done to ease the difficulties caused by professional boundaries. Formal process – agenda, reports, minutes – can lead to more time on paperwork, less on action. Plans devised at one step removed from the class teacher may appear acceptable for an individual child in isolation but not work in a particular class, given the dynamics of that group and the different demands they make on the teacher.

In my experience, the school, as the universal service for

Examples of the difficulties of joint working across public agencies

Example 1

A school arranged a meeting to agree next steps for Darren, a child with mobility difficulties. It is difficult to co-ordinate the diaries of the different people involved, in this case parents, child, class teacher, headteacher, psychologist, nurse, physiotherapist and doctor all are involved and need to be able to attend the meeting. At the meeting, little is achieved as the physiotherapist is on maternity leave and her replacement is off work ill. There is no physiotherapy assessment. The meeting is carried over for another two months.

Example 2

A ten year-old girl, Rita, was self-harming, but after GIRFEC assessment, targeted support worked well. One night the family left home secretly to avoid the mother's abusive partner, then moved again at which point Rita recommenced self-harming. Her new school had no information about the previous support arrangements. By the time local agencies had caught up with what was going on, Rita's family had moved once again across country to live near Rita's aunt.

---

all children, is the best location for many services dealing with children. I have seen multi-disciplinary professional teams, co-located in a shared office such as that in the North Inch Community Campus in Perth, develop effective quick informal ways of working together based around a shared commitment to put the child at the centre of their work, but the fact that some overcome professional and system barriers is no guarantee that all can. I have also seen the different professions within a local authority behave as rivals, bidding competitively for reducing budgets, guarding their turf, including their separate offices. From the class teacher's side of the desk, the resources provided seldom seem to match the identified needs – every child needs attention, not just those with 'additional needs'. In schools in less affluent areas, classes will often contain a higher number of children with additional needs or involved with GIRFEC processes. 'Working smarter' only goes so far. The choices are often longer working hours or spreading the jam more thinly. Across the country, GIRFEC and ASL are still works in progress.

From a different angle, the recent Jimmy Reid Foundation Report, 'Social Justice, The Common Weal and Children and Young People in Scotland'(2014) criticises GIRFEC (and the 2014 Children and Young People (Scotland) Act) as well-meaning but ineffective. Power relationships affect young people's lives. The report argues for more power for young people: a stronger statement of their rights; more opportunities for meaningful participation; less government 'performance targets' and more activities responding to the young people themselves. Tension between top-down and bottom-up is a central feature of democratic society, but in schooling there are too many top-down influences. This is explored further below, in the context of 'Standards' and the role of school inspectors.

Curriculum for Excellence reviewed

The first Curriculum for Excellence report, strong on principles and short on detail, was published in 2004, following issues raised in the National Debate on education of 2002. It stated that 'a significant proportion of young people in Scotland are not achieving all they are capable of.' It argued for a curriculum which would 'connect the various stages of learning from 3 to 18' and 'include a wide range of experiences and achieve a suitable blend of what has traditionally been seen as *academic and vocational.*'[21] Its purpose is to develop in Scotland's pupils the capacities to become 'successful learners, confident individuals, responsible citizens and effective contributors'. These ambitions received widespread support. In 2009, more details came in a large folder specifying 960+ essential 'learning experiences and outcomes' ('es' and 'os') covering ages 3 to 15, a period described as 'Broad General Education' (**BGE**). This 'exam-free zone' would allow teachers and pupils to deepen learning without the 'teach to the test' syndrome to which secondary schools in particular were said to default. Curriculum for Excellence also introduced health and well-being as a third essential component, alongside literacy and numeracy, of every child's curriculum.

The new curriculum encourages innovation and legitimates many worthwhile educational experiences which were seen by some as fringe activities outwith the real (i.e. examination) curriculum – global citizenship partnerships, eco-school activities, John Muir Awards, outdoor education, artistic performances and so on. Within Curriculum for Excellence, the process of learning becomes as important as the content, so it encourages classroom methods which help children to work together and learn with each other. These include co-operative learning, philosophy for kids, circle time and restorative approaches to conflict. Such collaborative approaches to learning help many children to learn better, as the examples which follow demonstrate, unlike the enforced silence of the classroom of yesteryear in which mute compliance was more valued than learning. So far so

---

Positive examples of Curriculum for Excellence in action

Children learn in different ways. In adult life, most work involves teams of people, with different strengths, working with and learning from each other. Many schools have 'restructured' traditional age-segregated class groups for some parts of the week with great success. When older and younger pupils get together, they can, as in families, learn from each other. Developments like this predate but are reinforced by the approach of Curriculum for Excellence. In several of the schools I visited on my tour, I saw examples of older and younger pupils working with each other. In St Bernadette's in Larbert, for example, where pupils from all years were working collaboratively on a joint task to develop proposals to improve the school grounds over the next three years. In many schools, 'real-life' challenges give children chances to learn and apply different skills – interviewing and consulting, recording and analysing results, mapping and investigating finance and practical issues in project planning.

Learning about the 'real world'

Peter runs a weekly 'philosophy' morning with his P6 class. The ten year-old pupils post ideas for their 'critical enquiry' on the 'philosophy wall' during the course of the week. From these they agree which topic to pursue. This morning it is 'free school meals' – why do some children get them and some don't? Within the first forty minutes of discussion, using well practised rules of how to contribute and when to listen, every class member has spoken. Issues of poverty, entitlement, universal benefits and social stigma have arisen. Using the smartboard, they do a search on school meals and discover the Children's Food Trust. Through its website they look at school meals in other countries. Every ten minutes, Peter asks the class to summarise the key points of the discussion and mindmaps these on the smartboard. This discussion led to the class, in separate teams, investigating the funding, social and nutritional advantages of various school meals. The class wrote a report, summarising the information they had discovered and stating their view that everyone should get free school meals, paid for by taxes. They sent this to their local councillors.

'Using skills from different 'subjects'

A staff team in a rural school community have worked with local partners (voluntary and businesses) to develop a range of 'community challenges' for pupils in the local High School. In two weeks freed up in the June school timetable, pupils worked in multi-age groups (12–15), supported by their teachers, to deliver on a standard format 'brief' (number involved, duration of project, costings etc). Projects include a village local history exhibition, a guide to the local area (in French, Spanish and English), tidying up a local church graveyard, clearing a local woodland. On the final day of the fortnight, short presentations are made by each 'team' on their project and local community leaders present awards to the pupils involved. In some cases, work on these challenges continues throughout the year.

good, but what happens when BGE meets the examination system?

After BGE, in S4, new national examinations (National 5), equivalent to Credit Level of Standard Grade, lead to Higher for those able to follow that route, giving stability to academic progression and standards. In 2014, ten years after the first report, 15 and 16 year olds up and down the country sat these new S4 examinations for the first time. For others, this so-called 'senior phase', post-15, is much less clear, with schools being encouraged to work with local partners (colleges, employers) to develop varied pathways for individual students.

Curriculum for Excellence, particularly in the Broad General Education phase, gives permission for innovation and new approaches to learning. Is it providing the best possible framework for learning for all Scotland's children? The Cabinet Secretary has recently agreed that the Scottish Government will commission independent evaluative research to answer this question, but it seems inevitable that this will evaluate only what can be 'measured'. How and at what age could you measure the extent to which someone is a 'responsible citizen'? Giving marks for 'confidence' might well end up being counterproductive. The new P7 and S3 profiles both aim to capture the quality of learning of each individual, but because they are individualised, they are difficult to aggregate into meaningful statistics. It will also be difficult to compare exam performance before and after 2014 reliably – for example, the different curriculum structures of Curriculum for Excellence mean that many S4 pupils are sitting examinations in fewer subjects.

Some statistics will be available. The Scottish Survey of Literacy and Numeracy (**SSLN**) (a *sample* of performance in literacy and numeracy at P4, P7 and S2) and the OECD's Programme of International Student Assessment (**PISA**) will over time allow some broad relatively reliable comparisons about the success, or otherwise, of Curriculum for Excellence in improving core learning skills in literacy and numeracy. Other useful statistics will be the numbers progressing on to Higher and to 'positive destinations' after school, but other factors than what is taught in school, such as local economic opportunity, also influence these figures. Another important area for evaluation is equity – if the effort, energy and money expended over more than ten years on Curriculum for Excellence does not address inequity, can it be said to have been worthwhile? A five year old who started Curriculum for Excellence in 2010 will not leave school till 2023. Reliable evaluation of the impact of Curriculum for Excellence statistically is going to take some time!

Meantime, both the process and design of Curriculum for Excellence have come in for criticism. Was it sensible to move all 2500+ Scottish schools into a new system, at the same time, irrespective of local circumstances and without prior piloting? This undoubtedly contributed to teachers' concerns about the overly bureaucratic approaches to curriculum planning in primary. In secondary, as Curriculum for Excellence moved up the school, it came to be completely dominated by the massive demands of bringing in the new examinations. Frequent changes in procedure and the overwhelming assessment workload of the new assessments in S4 led to high levels of worry and stress among teachers as well as pupils. How much did it cost in money and time? Could that money and time have been better spent in other ways? These questions hint at more general concerns with the management and governance arrangements of Scottish schooling picked up later in the book. While the Cabinet Secretary and the education establishment give out reassuring messages, teachers' surveys in 2013 and 2014, and a range of motions debated at their national conferences, tell a different story. There has also been some strong criticism, from different angles, of the design of Curriculum for Excellence. One of Scotland's leading educationists, Professor Mark Priestley, has argued that the design is confused, trying to do too many things and therefore in danger of not achieving any. Another, Professor Lindsay Paterson, has argued that the design abandons Scottish school education's commitment to a 'liberal education' for all pupils, while its content is insufficiently rigorous: a view echoed by some secondary teachers I know and respect who are worried that the content of the curriculum in subjects such as the sciences does not provide a sufficiently solid foundation for progression to Higher. Others have asked, 'why have we narrowed down to only six subjects at age 15?'

My own biggest concern is with the senior phase. The interface between BGE, with its open character, and the senior phase, dominated by examinations and credentials, has hardly been designed at all and this has led to great difficulties in planning progression and in some school timetables. I suspect that, despite the flurry of experiment with new timetable arrangements, when the dust settles not much will have changed. Those aiming for Higher have a long-established, well-understood programme leading to varied pathways beyond school. There is a common social understanding across the country about this route – it works well for Scotland and has been left, by and large, undisturbed. Once teachers get to grips with the new examinations, it is likely that, as in all previous curriculum changes, they will continue to see their first priority as providing secure progression to Higher in S4 and S5. Meantime, the ongoing inefficiencies of the Scottish sixth year, when many pupils who have obtained their university entrance qualifications in S5 lose momentum in their studies, remain untouched.

More worrying still, those who are less academically successful continue to have to navigate a more hazardous terrain than their Higher 'gold standard' peers. We are told that 'senior phase' will offer the right individual path for each, but, as we saw with Ian's experience, individuals can easily lose their way in what seems to be a difficult maze which neither the young person, nor their parents, nor the wider community, understand. Curriculum for Excellence, for all the work generated by it, does not yet seem to have set out a clear *national* plan to improve Ian's curricular experience. He, as much as Jim, was surely entitled to high status *national* recognition for his achievements at school in the senior phase. The task of developing alternative pathways for every young person, including Ian and his like, requires partnership across college, employers, careers advisers, voluntary sector, schools, training agencies, community organisations and parents. These need to be co-ordinated at a level beyond the individual school community, facilitated by clearer national curriculum design. I argue below that one of the features of such a design should be a high status route to a 'Scottish graduation certificate' open to all our pupils, one which would reflect some of the broader social and personal outcomes of Curriculum for Excellence, require core learning standards in literacy, numeracy and health and well-being and value achievement in community service, vocational and academic skills.

A final ongoing concern, threaded throughout this book, is that funding is clearly inequitable. Curriculum for Excellence values the 'whole child' not just the 'child in the classroom', yet clearly parental affluence, and the wider affluence of the immediate school community, plays a big part in determining access to learning activities beyond the classroom curriculum. Scotland has done well since 1997 in spending on the fabric and equipment of schools, but active learning experiences in, for example, the arts, outdoors or working in community, strongly encouraged in Curriculum for Excellence and remembered long after the work of the classroom has been forgotten, often require an element of private funding from parents. Behind outdoor learning challenges, residential experiences abroad, expert sports coaching, ski trips and the like lie transport costs, admission or residential charges, membership fees, equipment and music fees. The pattern is uneven across the country. In practice, schools often introduce 'informal' subsidies. Some local authorities fund more than others. Pupils in private schools have access to a wider range of privately funded learning activities that contribute greatly to the individual, but also to the sense of community and common purpose in the school community. Effectively, our state system has *privatised* these wider learning experiences – they are available mainly to those who can pay. Given all this, Curriculum for Excellence is still some way from delivering an excellent education for all children.

> **Issue #3:** Every child, irrespective of ability to pay, should have free access to a range of stimulating outwith classroom learning experiences, such as challenging experiences in specialist outdoor residential courses, throughout their school career.

School improvement reviewed

The Standards Act (2000) requires schools to improve constantly, and local authorities to evaluate that improvement. It arose from the commitment of the newly devolved Scottish Government that there should be no complacency in schooling policy – all schools would have to improve. On the surface, it gave parents, pupils and staff an important role in determining school priorities, but this has only ever been a token voice. Most of the power lies with local and national government and Her Majesty's Inspectorate of Education (**HMIE**), a group of educational experts to whom both local and national government defer. Individual school inspectors include some of the ablest hardest-working people I have ever met, passionately committed to getting the best for Scotland's children. Others, combining poor interpersonal skills with the overweening arrogance of those who are not themselves accountable, have used their power to damage rather than improve the Scottish system. I see similar positives and negatives in the system of inspections, wherein inspectors were both the creators of policy and the judges of its implementation: the policy is never wrong – people in schools just don't implement it well enough. Jack McConnell as Education Minister tried to limit their influence after their poor advice contributed to the crisis of the Scottish examination system in 2000. However, the inspection system has continued to dominate policy and practice because it defines what 'school improvement' is.

To 'improve' something is to 'make it better' but how can we judge if schooling is better? Statistics only take us so far. Many of the outcomes of Curriculum for Excellence, such as those of inclusion, are, as we have seen above, unmeasurable: they are found in the quality of the individual lives, not statistics about who attends which kind of school. The self-report of parents and/or pupils would give some information about quality, but there is no national system to collect these views reliably. I argue below that a main aim of school education is that children should learn to live in community – again there is no attempt made nationally to understand and liberate the concerns of school communities. Inspectors, alongside their observations, make use of statistics of the easily measurable – attendance, exclusion, positive destinations and, most of all, examination results – to 'rate' schools against 'performance indicators' of relative quality. Schools now often use these to measure their own progress each year. On the whole, if not taken to bureaucratic 'tick box' extremes, this can be a useful process, alongside, and giving equal weight to bottom-up discussions in the school community. However the power lies with the inspectors. It is their judgements and priorities that matter. That top-down pressure is hard to resist and effectively determines not just the priorities of schools but even the language used to describe what schooling is for. The lack of an independent appeal process means that, in practice, the answer to the old question 'who inspects the inspectors' is 'no-one', even though HMIE judgements have in the past been uneven in quality themselves. This lack of challenge to their version has blinded HMIE to weaknesses in their own process, regularly giving better ratings to secondary schools in affluent areas, for example, as if schools with a high proportion of poor pupils were somehow worse because they faced bigger challenges. This is like blaming doctors who work in the poorest areas for the earlier deaths of their patients. A further difficulty, acknowledged recently by a retired chief inspector, is that when inspections focus more on the school than the classroom, they oversimplify. Meantime the high-stakes public judgements about schools on a scale from 'excellent' to 'poor' often produce perverse unintended consequences rather than improvement.[22]

What's more, HMIE's improvement model of schooling is instrumental in its emphasis – schooling is designed to enhance economic competitiveness through improving specific out-comes, in particular examination results:

> Scotland's future economic prosperity requires an education system within which the population as a whole will develop the kind of knowledge, skills and attributes which will equip them personally, socially and economically to thrive in the 21st century. It also demands standards of attainment and achievement which match these needs and strengthen Scotland's position ...[23]

This neo-liberal concept of education at best took for

granted, or at worst neglected completely, the wider purposes of schooling outlined in the next chapter. Moreover, in focussing only on what schools and teachers do, it also neglected to give a full picture of the education of Scotland's children, an education in which schools and teachers play only a part.

HMIE's standardised approach has also stifled the very diversity and creativity that brings schools to life and which Curriculum for Excellence now seeks. Most schools and local authorities have followed their prescriptions, yet some of the biggest issues in Scottish school education, not least the different fates of Jim and Ian, outlined earlier, remain. In recent years, under new leadership, HMIE has shown a welcome recognition of complexity, and the judgements have become less 'precise' and more open in character. The inspection process will only play a useful role in supporting 'improvement' if it engages with the complexity of issues affecting schooling. The problems in a particular situation may not arise because schools are implementing their policies poorly (and so require punishment, blame, further advice, warnings). Perhaps the forces at work in that situation mean that the policy is unworkable in that specific situation. Research shows that very few policy prescriptions transfer readily from one school setting to another.[24] We need the right diagnosis to identify best situational options, school by school, rather than enforce a standardised top-down model in all circumstances – the last 'link in the chain' has to be guided locally not by the person at the far end of the chain. This is why Finland, the 'top performing' European system, has no inspectors but spends more money on improving the quality of every teacher in every classroom.

Like many headteachers before me, I would rather give a much stronger voice to the parents and pupils of a school community than to inspectors who have provided standardised prescriptions for all schools, who have in the past judged quality on the basis of how well their own limited recommendations are being implemented. When as a headteacher I listened to parents talking about what they wanted for their children from school education, they often mentioned standards, but they would also express other types of wants – 'I want her to grow up happy', 'I want her to have good friends,' 'I want him to be able to get a secure job'. These kinds of 'wants' are echoed in the pragmatic and sensible judgements which pupils make about their futures, memorably demonstrated in the English research of Hoskins and Barker in their recent report on how academies fail to increase pupils' aspirations.[25] These outcomes will never be delivered by an education system based around narrow competitive individualism, rating every child on a linear comparative scale of success. They require education in communities of equal respect, in schools which value what every child brings, not just how well he or she can perform.

Issue #4: Scotland needs a system of annual online standardised surveys of all teachers, parents and pupils to balance the 'performance' concerns of national government with the voice of the local school community. In such a system, the grass roots voice of the local community would have an equal say in determining how a school is run.

Ironically, despite putting 'performance' at the top of the schooling agenda, Scotland's school improvement system provides only limited data on performance. Schools and teachers, primary and secondary, need to benchmark the work of their pupils against national standards as part of the evaluation of their work. A new benchmarking system for secondary schools has been under development to coincide with the introduction of the new examination system and will benefit from current piloting and evaluation. However there is no standardised benchmarking for primary school attainment.

Every child in Scotland should attain, with additional support if required, a high level of basic literacy (including communicative competence) and numeracy before leaving primary school, and should maintain and enhance that competence in the first three years of secondary. This is a minimum threshold level below which their capacity for autonomous living is threatened. Current arrangements for moderated internal assessments by class teachers do not give either parents or teachers sufficiently robust data on this vital area. This is a foundational responsibility of primary schools. All Scotland should speak of this as the child's entitlement, as important as child protection, or good health, or any of the GIRFEC 'SHANARRI' areas. Standardised tests of literacy and numeracy are a quick, efficient and contextually-neutral way of assessing progress, widely used in some authorities, but not currently a requirement. Ministers are rightly wary of standardised testing after Michael Forsyth's attempt to impose it in the early 1990s – the campaign against his proposals became a high point of pre-devolution civic democracy. The main objection was that test results would be used to set up a 'schools market' based on league tables, to judge rather than to help pupils' progress. My argument is not for a 'market', based on results aggregated at school level, but for confidential individual testing, at key points in the primary school, on the medical model.

Standardised measurement in literacy and numeracy can check local expectations against international standards, alerting all concerned to slow development, encouraging appropriate support, stimulating corrective actions. Test results should be individual and confidential to the child, the teacher and the parent and never seen as part of a competition or individual comparison. Parents and children should be full partners in discussion and in subsequent plans, particularly if additional support or recovery programmes are required. There should be no blame attached to restorative interventions any more than to medical interventions. Each child's progress, in literacy in particular, is too important to cover up when they are falling far behind. We need a 'New Deal' for literacy and numeracy in an expanded partnership of school, home and community. A similar testing arrangement for health and well-being, involving periodic self evaluation against standardised measures and encouragement to plan balanced improvements, might be more politically controversial but would give a structured space within which to engage parents and children about childhood obesity and other legitimate health concerns.

Issue #5: All primary school children should benefit from knowing how they are performing in standardised tests of literacy and numeracy, and take part in health and well-being assessments, including elements of structured self assessment. These should be confidential to child, parent and teacher and discussed annually in a confidential session, where parent, child and teacher plan relevant next steps and, if necessary, access appropriate recovery programmes.

CHAPTER THREE

Learning and living in community

Foundations of democratic life – liberty, equality, community

Schools reflect and contribute to democratic life, not the democracy of 'Big Politics' – elections, budgets and new laws – but the democracy of respect, responsibility and rights, the '3Rs' of everyday life. For the American political philosopher Robert Dahl, democratic life is a constant balancing act between social forces and beliefs that emphasise individual freedom and autonomy and those which emphasise compromise and social control.[26] These are not just issues for government or political theory. This balancing act can be found at all levels in all the social functions and experience of plural democracies. As outlined in Chapter One, freedom and equality find different balance points in a schooling system – the diversity of interests, talents and values of a plural society require great freedom but greater freedoms increase inequality as those already advantaged use their advantages to gain even more. We saw above how parental choice enhances the 'freedom' of parents against the potential 'control' of the state. However the best route for one individual may restrict the choices of another. This is where the third democratic principle comes in – what the political theorist Bernard Crick calls 'the forgotten value of fraternity.'[27] 'Fraternity' puts liberty and equality into practice. It involves empathy and emotion. It is about personal relationships, interacting with other people in real places and real time. It is harder to be disrespectful when you are face to face and can see someone's reaction to what you say. The politician who bullies his own staff is no democrat, no matter how much he goes on, in high-flown speeches, about equality and freedom. Fraternal relationships of warmth and concern are a necessary part of democratic living. Fraternity is not just a principle, but a key purpose of democracy. Liberty and equality are, if taken to extremes, socially damaging – each needs the other to be kept in balance. Fraternity is the means as well as the end. It is found in abundance in our diverse comprehensive school communities. Where children live and work together face-to-face, as in the comprehensive neighbourhood school, they learn from as well as with each other.

But there is a problem with the actual word 'fraternity,' which is perhaps why it's not used much nowadays. It only refers to men. Women are excluded. Michael Fielding, who has written with great insight on schooling and democracy, coins the term 'democratic fellowship' to replace 'fraternity', but for me 'fellowship' has an equally archaic, masculine and exclusive ring to it. I prefer the term 'community'. Although it is a loose open concept, much used and abused, it catches the intimacy of democratic social life. In communities, people collaborate and co-operate, they recognise each other's needs, they negotiate around conflict and difference, they have a sense of belonging, a shared identity. There is a danger that communities can become introverted, exclusive, insular, concerned with boundaries, while communities are seldom without their own conflicts. Within small communities, bullying, resentments and spites are as common as collaboration and care. Communities therefore need the universal values of freedom and equality to balance out their inward exclusiveness – an outward-facing recognition of others, not the introverted defensiveness of 'here's tae us, wha's like us?' We have passed the phase in our society of rushing to the barricades. Our challenge is how to live together though our values and interests differ and schools are the first place in which we learn about that kind of living together, beyond the bubble of our family, our friendships, our interests.

The school as a democratic community

The constant balancing of liberty and equality can be found everywhere in schools – a space where the values of community and the bonds of the family are taken out into wider society and learned and practised daily. In diverse 21st century democratic societies, individuals participate in many purposeful 'communities' of different types – virtual and real, geographically-based or at long-reach, work-based and friendship-based, values-based and interest-based. Some of these 'communities' may be restricted by exclusive membership rules, or a limited task or interest-based focus – worthwhile in their own terms but neither inclusive nor democratic. Schools, particularly comprehensive schools, are uniquely well-placed to give pupils an experience of what 'democratic community' means. It is in the school that the growing child meets social diversity, differing values and interests, and understands how to live with difference. The school community[28] is a step into the more impersonal wider plural society – a society of social divisions, competing values and potentially clashing interests. The school system can bring people together within a purposeful whole or maintain, or even create, division, allocating people to different places, different roles, offering some routes to fulfilment and closing others down, renewing or fragmenting community, tolerating abuse, unfairness and bullying or using such conflict to model and teach better ways. Schools model in microcosm the relationships of adult society by the different ways in which they engage with these challenges of contemporary living.

The Scottish philosopher John Macmurray argued powerfully in the 1957 Moray House lecture that the primary purpose of education is that of how to live in community:

> ... the first priority in education – if by education we mean learning to be human – is learning to live in personal relation to other people. Let us call it learning to live in community. I call this the first priority because failure in this is fundamental failure, which cannot be compensated for by success in other fields; because our ability to enter into fully personal relations with others is the measure of our humanity ... the greatest threat to education in our own society [is that] ... gradually we are falling victims to the illusion that all problems can be solved by proper organisation; that if we fail it is because we are doing the job in the wrong way, and that all that is needed is 'the know-how'. To think thus in education is to pervert education. It is not an engineering job. It is personal and human.[29]

In the school community and its relationship to the wider community, the child learns about his or her relationship to others, how he or she fits in, or does not, what kinds of behaviour are sanctioned, whom to trust. A developing 'sense of community', and the personal identity that goes along with it, can help create meaning and value in life. Where there is a 'sense of community' in the school, pupils, staff and parents share a common purpose. This is not the democracy of elected representatives and party conflict, but the democracy of respect, equal personal dignity, mutual trust or mistrust. The relationships it generates affect children's social development and also their learning.

Motivation to learn

Motivation to learn is both individual (internal) and social (external) in character. Pupils develop a concept of themselves as more or less successful learners, through their experience of schooling and learning experiences outside school, as we saw in Chapter 1 with Jim and Ian. The influential Scottish educational psychologist Alan McLean identifies three '3 As' as constituent elements of motivation in learning in his book *The Motivated School* (2003).[30] The first, **Agency,** expresses the level of confidence an individual has to act on what they see as their own individual free choices. When children experience success in learning, their confidence grows and they want to learn more. Some pupils with high agency in other areas reject school. They may be part of a gang sub-culture or have future work intentions that don't involve school – school is not for them; 'forcing' them to learn may lead to vigorous, or undercover, resistance.

McLean's second 'A', **Affiliation,** has a social character – how much does a pupil associate him or herself with the school community? Recent research by the University of London demonstrates the strength of the relationship between school achievement and identification with the norms, values and aims of the school. In more traditional societies, increased motivation may be encouraged by external forces – common cultural norms or even physical force (as we did in Scotland until the early 1980s with 'the belt'). I have taught in classrooms in East Asia and found much higher levels of commitment to school education among many families there, alongside higher expectations of social conformity and higher levels of social and political control of the lives of individuals, adult and child, in wider society. Although this generally produces more pliable respectful pupils, East Asian social conformity sits uneasily with the diversity and individualism valued in Western culture – a different cultural balance point between freedom and control.

The third A is **Autonomy** – that word again – a key aim of school education and democratic society more generally. Autonomous learners are self-motivated and have acquired skills to learn by themselves. McLean shows how pupils with different levels of agency and affiliation adopt different 'learning stances' – 'focussed', 'hiding', 'stroppy', 'angry'. This affects their autonomy as learners for good or ill. The 'learning stances' frame pupils' attitude to school learning.

From a different angle, the American psychologist Carol Dweck also demonstrates that *how* you think affects what you think is *possible*: some individuals have a 'growth' mindset believing that individual capacities can be developed and improved.[31] Others hold a 'fixed' mindset believing that capacities are limited for ever. Many children acquire a fixed view of their own capacities during school, often through comparing themselves with others – 'I'm no good at maths', 'I canny run for toffee', 'I'm dozy', 'I'm not brainy'. Motivation thus has a social element – it is affected by the relationships of the classroom, the school, the wider community. As pupils approach the senior phase of secondary school, it is increasingly affected by pupils' perception of how their school experience, and the 'credentials' they may obtain, fit with their thinking about which pathways are open to them beyond school, who they think they will become in society.

The 'hidden curriculum' of the school community and the schooling system

The formal policies of schooling – inclusion, support, CforEx, quality standards – contain many worthy words. But policies are not practice. Schools communities have a 'hidden curriculum' where pupils learn – both in class and in the daily exchanges of school life – about life beyond the family and their street, about rights and responsibilities, fairness and justice, prejudice, crime and punishment, options for adult life and employment. Only in school are individuals compelled to share so much of their lives in a crowded space, with a random cross-section of society – a gated community, with its own work ethic, routines and rules. Each age-segregated socially diverse class is locked together in compulsory attendance for 190 days a year and exposed to the ruthless social competitiveness of the peer group: who is a better fighter, has more fashionable clothes, is more attractive, is best at mathematics, or will go on to occupations which are more valuable or important? In meeting the social challenges of school, children internalise messages about their social value – where they fit in to these informal social pecking orders. Learning outside the classroom – the liberating freedom of lunchtime with friends, the sniggering jibes of a bully – can mean more in a child's growing life than any number of mathematical equations or science experiments.

In these social exchanges and relationships, pupils compare themselves to others, learn how others see them, what others value in them. In Curriculum for Excellence, every pupil is said to have equal value. In the hidden curriculum that may not be true. The labels 'credit' and 'foundation' in Standard Grade were, for example, meant to be neutral descriptions of different levels, but 'credit' carries overtones of comparatively higher worth than 'foundation' and the labels were quickly transferred by some pupils, teachers and parents to the children themselves – a 'foundation class', a 'credit pupil'. Some pupils study 'Highers' – in some subliminal sense does this make them 'higher' in other respects? As a headteacher, I regularly talked with talented young people who, lacking the particular skills required to succeed at Credit Level, were demotivated by an exam system in which they felt they could never achieve well. There are hundreds of these kinds of 'below the radar' valuations in the daily language and practices of schools.

The hidden curriculum is taught not by lessons in classrooms but by words used as labels, by systems that order and categorise. Everything that happens in the school community – from informal personal greetings to organisational processes –

expresses particular values, particular views about relationships, about who should have power, who should have a voice, and why. Pupils learn from the hidden messages of the funding model of Curriculum for Excellence. For example, do they have to pay for certain activities? What's optional or compulsory? Does the school assume that they have a broadband connection at home?

Pupils not only learn from their relationships with the different people of the school community – teachers and school bus drivers, cleaners and cooks, headteachers and classroom assistants, but also from the relationships these adults have with each other. Are these relationships functional or personal, respectful or bullish, warm or cold? Who gets paid most, who gets paid least? This is where they learn what the school stands for – not in its words. Since school is often the first and most significant place where they encounter a cross section of wider society, they learn by extension where they fit in society as a whole – how society works for them. They also learn how organisations function – why some people get paid more than others, why some have more power and how they use it, and what records are kept. Some of these 'messages' are the very frames of their social experience.

Functional institutions or personal communities?

Michael Fielding, following Macmurray, places the personal goals of schools above their functional goals.[32] He is critical of the way in which schools, nationally (and internationally, through for example PISA), have been put under increasing pressure to put 'performance' above people. Where this happens, pupils are there simply to achieve 'results'. Pupils, he argues, should always be more than 'performance units' in an all-consuming quest for global economic efficiency. Functional and personal are both necessary – if the balance is right they can reinforce each other, but where the personal is used *for* the functional, individuals (staff and/or pupils) have value only as they contribute to the overall function of the school (higher examination results etc). Pressure to put the functional (pupils as units in a performance-based culture) above the personal is very real in today's schools. My book on the 'dilemmas' faced by headteachers in today's schools shows how these, and similar pressures, make for hard choices in the lives of teachers and individual children.[33]

Trust – the glue of school communities

The importance of trust, not just performance, was always on my mind as a headteacher. I have seen high levels of mutual trust in many of the schools I have worked in. In my school tour I saw some outstanding examples of the common endeavour and mutual respect of community in the schools I visited. 'Wee Pans' is a great example of a school where there are no walls between home, school and community. In Auchenharvie in North Ayrshire, pupils shared with me how they influenced community discussions about their possible merger with Ardrossan Academy. They spoke warmly of the 'skills' sessions in their curriculum when the functional requirements of the examination syllabus gave way to a more personal engagement between pupil and pupil, pupil and teacher. In the North Inch Community Campus in Perth, I saw evidence of a faith school reaching out to, and including, its secular geographical community rather than building defences and exclusivity. In Bucksburn in Aberdeen, I saw pupils bringing the local business community into productive dialogue about energy needs and provision in the longer term. These examples showed schools helping to 'build community', echoing the themes of community empowerment and renewal which Alf and Ewan Young observed in their journey round Scotland in their 'Postcard from Scotland' – *The New Road* (*2012*).

Sense of community is based on mutual trust – the glue that holds a community together. Individuals are constantly making judgements about the motivations of others through observation of how they behave as well as what they say. While trust can be built by consistency and fairness in the little unspoken exchanges of daily living, it can easily be lost if power is used unfairly, if teacher behaviour or the impersonal systems of the school appear disrespectful, or if motives are misinterpreted. Without trust, the bonds of community are weakened and the authority of the school community is diminished. Where pupils do not trust the school, its systems and teachers, they may withdraw into a grudging compliance, waiting for the day when they can leave, or worse, adopting a hostile attitude, in words or behaviour, which drags their school life, and sometimes that of those around them, into a negative spiral. In the example which follows, there is no trust between teacher and pupil, consequently Sarah feels no obligation either to the school or the teacher. She justifies her behaviour by what she sees as the unfair way in which she has been treated.

Democratic principles in conflict – freedom, control, exclusion, inclusion

In Brasenose Academy, the policy of 'banning' smartphones was widely seen as out of date, unworkable and uneducational, given their potential to be used as a 'computer in the pocket'. After a community-wide debate in which the various advantages and concerns of their use in school were aired in the Parent Forum, through the Student Council, and in staff meetings, pupils were allowed to use phones in social areas outwith the timetabled school day or in class for educational purposes agreed with the teacher (e.g. looking up online references or downloading notes from the smartboard). Teachers could apply sanctions such as confiscation to discourage abuse, e.g. recording the teacher at work or distracting texting.

Jean, a depute headteacher, was called to a heated argument in a science laboratory. Sarah, a 14 year old pupil, had been using her mobile phone under the desk but, when asked to hand it over, confronted the teacher angrily and refused to do so or even to leave the room to discuss the issue in a less confrontational one-to-one. Both Sarah and the teacher were very upset. The learning objective of the lesson (to learn how to balance simple neutralisation equations) was long gone. Jean took Sarah away to calm her down. When Sarah's mother came in for a discussion about the incident, she stuck up for Sarah who, she said, was justified in disrupting the class because 'she needed to have her phone cos her cousin in Wales was ill' and that the teacher had been 'unfair'. Sarah explained, 'Kirsten used her phone and the teacher did nothing about it'. 'She's never liked me anyway' and 'I didn't want to take science in the first place, the school made me do it.' Later on, another pupil told Jean that

Sarah had actually been texting round to arrange a confrontation with another girl that she had been told flirted with her (Sarah's) boyfriend.

In this conflict of values and interests can be found the complex political and interpersonal reality of life in a plural school community – trust and mistrust, feelings of fairness and 'hidden injuries' lie beneath the emotional exchanges of such disputes. The functional work of the school (the science lesson) is disrupted. For the teacher this was about fairness and equality for the rest of the class – disruptive pupils should not prevent others learning ('they want to learn from me, I'm here to teach science not to deal with this kind of stuff'); for Jean this was about guarding the floodgates – there are some issues she would rather keep outside (a strong reminder went out to the whole school about use of social media in school); for Sarah's social worker (contacted under GIRFEC rules) the school should work harder to reduce Sarah's 'at-risk' behaviour (she had been cautioned for assault before); for Sarah's mother this was a chance to stand up for, rather than argue with, her daughter; for Sarah herself this was just another example of why she wanted to leave school at the first opportunity. She was desperate for adult freedom.

This example is adapted from Murphy, D. (2012), 'Democratic schooling: past, present and future' in Brown et al (eds) *Democratic Citizenship in Schools*, Edinburgh: Dunedin Academic Press.

At one level, Sarah's disruptive behaviour is a choice she is making. At another level, it reflects her view of the school – an oppressive institution, illegitimate in its claims to authority and commanding no loyalty. Older 'misbehaving' pupils like Sarah may find words to justify antisocial behaviour in terms of earlier unfair or disrespectful treatment they believe they experienced; with younger children there is often simply emotional behaviour.

Such rejection of the authority of the school as an institution can also transfer to the authority of the teacher as an 'expert'. Pupils who mistrust the school system because, as they see it, it disrespects them in some way often also reject the authority of school knowledge as well. For them education's emancipatory potential has been lost. School education seems like a system of induction into a 'priestly code', conferring privileges on its initiates, those who achieve relative success, and condemning those who cannot hope for such success to paths which the school proclaims to be less valuable. As a teacher and headteacher, I met many very able pupils who loved study, engaged freely with the great disciplines of learning and were highly self-motivated. I also met many for whom schooling was a means to an end – to acquire the qualifications needed to go and do something else in the 'real world'. Many saw schooling as an experience done *to* them, rather than *with* and *for* them. School was at best to be tolerated as an experience that would soon be finished, or at worst an experience that was obstructive and harmful to the person they wanted to be.

Richard Sennett and Jonathan Cobb, in their classic study of white working class Bostonian men, *The Hidden Injuries of Class* (1972), demonstrated how, in a society which gives respect according to 'ability', it is easy for those who are deemed to be 'less able' to resent it and to feel disrespected. The men they studied were materially wealthy enough, with all the luxuries of modern living, and yet in some there was a 'hidden injury' that they had not been dealt a fair deal. The resentments, anger and frustrations that coloured their adult lives started in how they felt they had been treated at school. I have not conducted such in-depth studies of children, but forty years of experienced observation in many schools tells me that these hidden messages are among the most important ones a school gives its pupils. Very often particular incidents are less important than a general sense of the unfairness of society as a whole, an unfairness which justifies an 'aggressive defensive' posture – 'there's no-one else to stick up for me so I have to stick up for myself.' Where parents feel themselves unfairly treated in an unfair society, it is no surprise that their children may come to view school as another oppressive institution, controlling rather than liberating.

School regulations constantly try to find a workable balance between individual freedoms, the social conformity required by the classroom and the practicalities of life when a large number of people are crowded together, moving back and forward many times a day in a small space. Sarah might just as easily have got into an argument about any rule – what she was wearing, where she was walking, whether she had brought a pencil or homework book. Unstated feelings of unfairness, underlying conflicts between individual freedom and imposed conformity, often underpin conflicts such as this example.

Is the school expecting enough of Sarah? What levers does the school have to expect more from her? Any punishment – detention, exclusion – will increase her alienation, exacerbating feelings of being treated unfairly. The prospect of working harder for examinations simply to confirm that she is in the 'bottom half' is not appealing. I have seen many 'Sarahs' dig in for continuing confrontation when faced with top-down demands, either in particular classrooms or in school in general. I have also seen 'Sarahs' transformed when, instead of being forced into a curriculum which they have rejected, the teacher or the school listens to them and creates learning spaces where they can find relative success. Expectations matter but so does care. Care, concern and compassion, and the trusting relationships they create, can soften these conflicts. Steven Quinn, former headteacher at Auchenharvie, like many successful headteachers, spoke to me of his philosophy of 'tough love', the teacher as a strict but caring parent, the school as a family with high expectations. Being tough without the love is disrespectful, disempowering. Without 'the love', the pupil is a cog in the machine. Age also makes a difference – it is easier to 'care' more with younger children. Sarah may have learned already, by age 14, that she cannot trust anyone in authority any more.

Realising the four capacities of Curriculum for Excellence – responsible citizenship, successful learning, active contributions and individual confidence – is not just a task for individuals but for the community. It is a challenge for which primary schools are better suited than the typically bigger, less personal, secondary schools, closer to an adult world of social division and inequality. Nonetheless, many Scottish secondary schools as well as primary, like those I report on in my school tour, generate a positive energy about the future, their community life uplifting and empowering. Why can't all schools do this for all their pupils? Laying all the responsibility on the individual school masks the depth and complexity of the factors involved. Every level of the schooling system – home, classroom, school, local and national – has to work together to realise democratic values of fairness and equality of respect in each school. Some schools have many fewer resources, not just material resources but 'community capital', accumulated resources of trust: trust that the system of which the school is a part cares enough about and will be able to deliver for each of its pupils. Trust in the value of school education is something that schools in more affluent areas have in abundance.

It was only as a depute headteacher, then later as a headteacher much more strongly, that I understood that the institution of the school can also be vulnerable, and that some school communities are much stronger than others. Building consensus, sharing values, comfortable acceptance of familiar routines build strength and resilience, and 'organisational capital'. These in turn bring consistency – trust comes not just because you like every aspect of what the school does, or because you trust the individuals, but because you know *what* you are dealing with. In contrast, schools experiencing social pressures, organisational weaknesses, poor leadership or badly managed change, or where pupils do not see the school helping them in their real lives, can quickly go into a negative spiral of instability, internal contention and strife. Where trust is diminished and social cohesion reduced, it's 'each for himself'. Each individual, losing trust in the institution, fights for his or her own space. The school as a community fragments with damaging effects on all its members, staff and pupils alike. In a community where everyone puts their own individual interests above that of the organisation, everyone loses out. One of the headteacher's jobs is to avoid this kind of implosion, to maintain the stability of the school as an organisation. This is an unrecognised task, much easier in some school settings than in others – and it is the headteacher who is in charge, isn't it?

CHAPTER FOUR

Who is in charge of schooling?

Many people see the headteacher as the ultimate authority in a school, both responsible and accountable for what happens, whereas headteachers, as the report on 'recruitment and retention' cited below makes clear, sometimes feel less in control than charting a perilous path between the competing forces of top-down policy and bottom-up reality: teachers, parents and pupils stubbornly refuse to fit into the neat prescriptions in the tens of thousands of pages and online 'pdfs' of policy – headteachers have power, but so do many others in the school and outside it. In the classic hierarchical organisational model of private business, responsibilities are clearly defined and accountability ultimately feeds back to a clear 'bottom line'. In school education, there are many 'bottom lines', defined by many different players in the system – responsibility is diffuse and accountability consequently confused. The 'official' account tells only part of the story.

The 'official' account

The 'official' view of democratic governance is that citizens, through voting and paying taxes, exercise ultimate power over all public services. Politicians can be removed from power – they are the servants of the electorate. While in office they exercise power over paid officials, such as civil servants, who collect the taxes and manage the work, or public expert professionals such as doctors, teachers or nurses, who 'do the work'. This way of thinking was emphasised in the reforms of the Thatcher era when the public sector was redefined as a sort of market place of 'services'.

In some respects this is an accurate picture. Ultimate power rests with 'big politics', which has the capacity to effect system-wide institutional change. The continuing impact of the educational reforms begun in 1965 is a good example, and the 1990s policies of market-place choice and competition in public service another. In other ways this version is too simple. School systems have been described as 'loosely coupled' – the 'outcomes' of schooling are a long way from the initial inputs.[34] Pushing a chain leads to unpredictable outcomes – the longer the chain, the less likely that the final link will move in the intended direction. The official account conceals as much as it reveals. Ask yourself who is responsible, who is accountable and who *should* be accountable for the different decisions made and the different outcomes reached in the fictional examples below. They show how the neat lines of responsibility of the official account are messed up by the complexity of life in the school community.

Figure A: Responsibility and accountability in public service

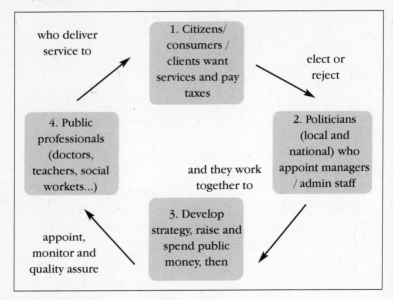

In these messy parts of school life, described more fully in my book about the 'dilemmas' of the headteacher, one person's view of what is at stake is radically different from another's. Interests and values clash and local sources of power can outmuscle distant national policies. However detailed the national guidance, it never matches the complexity of specific situations. When national or local politicians or their officials get too involved in the detail, and start prescribing what to do, they often lack context-sensitive understanding, nor may they see the day-to-day impact of their decisions on individuals.

Who is responsible?

Who then is responsible for what happens in Scotland's schools? It is true that the Scottish Government (SG) sets policy and provides strategic direction. It also acts through national agencies such as the Scottish Qualifications Agency (SQA) and Education Scotland (ES), which includes the Inspectors. Scotland's 32 multi-purpose local authorities run the schools and employ the teachers, but are dependent on SG for funding (only around 15 per cent of local authority income is from Council Tax).

Who is responsible?

Example 1

Arlene, an English teacher in St. Perpetua Academy, arranged an evening theatre trip for a group of S4 pupils to see a dramatisation of Steinbeck's Of Mice and Men. She decided that Jason, one of the class, cannot go on the trip because he has misbehaved in her class repeatedly. The headteacher receives a complaint from Jason's father that his son is 'being discriminated against because of his behaviour difficulties', but upholds Arlene's decision – Jason is 'at risk' because he cannot be trusted to follow Arlene's instructions off site. Jason's father complains to one of his MSPs who writes to the Council, querying the decision on the basis of the father's account. The Council leader instructs the Director of Learning and Leisure to investigate and report. She delegates the task to the Head of Schools, Alan, who decides that Jason must be allowed to go on the trip and so informs the father. When the headteacher tells Arlene the decision, she cancels the trip. 'This is not part of my job but something I chose to do in

---

my own time', she says. Alan then rewords the Council's guidance on extra-curricular activities to make clear that all children must have these opportunities, but the teacher associations, in discussion at the Council's 'Joint Negotiating Committee' meeting, block this move. They successfully persuade the councillors that it is better to let this sleeping dog lie. Issuing a new policy may result in many teachers withdrawing altogether from extra-curricular activities. Meantime Arlene's pupils miss their evening at the theatre and the other parents and pupils don't know why, as all these exchanges took place behind closed doors.

Example 2

Stantonshire Council gives support to children whose first language is not English through its English as an Additional Language Service (**EAL**). A teacher, who taught some children at Headwall Primary School, left the service and has not been replaced for budget reasons. Amy, a Headwall teacher with a lead role in EAL, discovers after summer that the council recruited a new EAL teacher to teach in a new high profile reception centre for asylum seekers. She complained to her headteacher: 'I am the only one who sees the impact on the children.' But the head has already argued with her director and was told that supporting asylum seekers was the highest political priority. Amy wants to contact the local press to inform the public. She believes the wider civic community should have the chance to discuss the issue. However her contract of employment prevents her from speaking critically of the Council so she stays silent.

Example 3

The Pinmill area 'Community Learning Team' arranged exciting free after-school leisure activities for 'young offenders', meeting them with a minibus each Wednesday outside Pinmill Academy at the end of the school day. Their aim was to 'reach out to the most challenging young people in the community' to help to reduce offending. The Student Council, backed by the Parent Council, wrote to the local authority, incensed that some of the 'worst behaved' pupils were being 'rewarded for bad behaviour'. As they saw it, 'it seems that the worse behaved you are, the more you get'. Issues of 'equality' and 'fairness' were to the fore in subsequent discussions. The Student Council would not accept the arguments of the Council official who came out from 'Head Office' to persuade them otherwise.

Despite party political differences, SG seldom demands more than local authorities are willing to give. There is usually a commitment to reach consensual decisions – East Renfrewshire's decision to 'break ranks' by postponing the introduction of the new examinations to 2015 was unusual. While debates on education in the Scottish Parliament are often of high quality and MSPs are generally, in my experience, better informed on educational policy than their local equivalents and very accessible at Holyrood and in schools, MSPs are not the government and do not run the schools.

Scotland is a small country. Key players – ministers from SG, senior civil servants, HMIE, COSLA (the Convention of Scottish Local Authorities), ADES (the Association of Directors of

Education in Scotland) and SQA – know each other and meet regularly. Teacher associations, particularly the EIS with over 80 per cent of Scotland's teachers as members, also regularly sit at the 'top table'. Unlike in England, where passionate disagreements are daily aired in the media, potential problems are often defused behind closed doors, in phone calls, through informal consultations with these 'key players'. Special interest groups, charities, parent associations, employers' organisations, universities and colleges all play a role in contributing to national schooling policy, but carry much less political weight when decisions are made. Detailed policy development is often delegated to national working groups, such as the Curriculum for Excellence Management Board, with members chosen to represent the powerful insiders. Although Scotland therefore doesn't have the frenetic turbulence of English educational policy making, the insider discussions of the Scottish policy community often leaves the civic community behind. We catch up later without the benefit of the private negotiations which led to their compromise agreements. For many in a school community, such policy development is remote. The gap between policy intention and life in schools, most visible in this book in the failure to close the gap between Ian and Jim, Catherine and Elaine, is why many argue that Scotland needs to reconsider its arrangements for school governance.

Over the last thirty years, English policy has diverged greatly. There, government has removed power from local authorities, increased the autonomy of individual schools and given parents and inspectors more power to hold schools to account. Scotland shares some elements of this 'school improvement' agenda, yet there are few voices in Scotland in favour of similar reforms up here. Local authorities guard jealously their school budgets and have considerable successes in their management of school education. There were many examples on my school tour – the strategic vision and hard work that led to the outstanding community school hubs in Perth and Kinross, the plan for the new Caol community learning campus, Falkirk's 'Learning to Achieve' policy. In my last job at Lornshill, I regularly saw that no-one cares as much about Clackmannanshire, or listens as much to its people, as the local councillors who live there and who devote their lives to its service. On the other hand, despite the quality of its *people*, there is much cogent, if muted, criticism of the inhibiting effects of the present local government *system*. For example:

- small local authorities, with multiple responsibilities and tight budgets, can lack capacity to give school education the attention it deserves;

- in some authorities, where Chief Executives and Strategic Directors lack specialist schooling expertise, bureaucratic management practice replaces sensitive local decision-making;

- there are significant variations in spending on schools – inputs are very unequal across the country. With Audit Scotland reporting a 9 per cent real terms reduction in education spending since 2010 and further cuts coming, budget pressures will increase;[35]

- the system is wasteful, with around[36] 32 sets of officials, 32 'joint negotiating committees' for teachers' conditions, 32 similar policies on 'inclusion' written by 32 different local committees.

A recent influential report by the Commission on School Reform, 'By Diverse Means' (2013) argued that current governance arrangements hold back innovation – that Scottish schooling needs to be diversified if it is to meet the challenges of the future:

> … the system is too uniform. It lacks the diversity that is a vital element of any learning organisation. The Commission sees the promotion of increased variety in the system as a crucially important prerequisite of future improvement. The best way of achieving this objective is to increase the autonomy of individual schools. Every school … should be encouraged to innovate and take well-considered risks. At present, however, schools are reluctant to take the initiative. This is because the culture of the system as a whole is disempowering.[37]

Despite the excellent work of many councillors and officials in local authorities, working hard every day to keep the system on track, the report is surely right that the present system has reached its limit. The looming funding crisis adds to the argument. The independence debate has focussed attention on national government, but surely at some point present local government arrangements must be reviewed again.

Where governance is devolved entirely to the individual school, however, as in the English 'academies' model, there is a real danger of further increasing inequality. Schools with high numbers of children from less affluent backgrounds struggle to keep up with more affluent schools, which, like private schools, can call on a reservoir of social advantages in the school and its wider community – advantaged schools attract advantaged parents who find ways to get the system to work better for their children. Any new governance system must not abandon socially disadvantaged communities to the bottom of a competitive pile. We should consider a number of options and perhaps pilot and experiment with these before making a change across the whole country. One such option is that the human services, namely health, school and college education, community care and social work could be run jointly. The closest potential partners of 32 education authorities are the 13 college regions and 14 health boards – why not align the borders of these major human services to help them work better together in 14 directly elected boards, with the power to raise taxes hypothecated for education and health? These would be light touch bodies with regulatory planning and support functions, within a framework of national standards, matched, in the case of schooling, by local level accountabilities as outlined below. If community level professionals from all these agencies were working together, as in the best GIRFEC examples, this would do much to bring coherence to the educational experience of children whose contact with public agencies may currently be episodic or even incoherent. The combination of this kind of authority with greater voice for the parents and pupils of each school would provide a much better balance of strategic and professional support alongside local ownership than the current 32, or the 100 small multipurpose authorities of the kind proposed in August 2014 by COSLA's Commission on Strengthening Local Democracy.

The restrictiveness of current governance is not just to do with local authorities. The powerful, top-down prescriptions of the school inspectorate have made the Scottish schooling system remarkably uniform in character but diminished the role of teachers and headteachers. The London Challenge showed that when schools are given considerable devolved powers, but work collaboratively within a supportive professional network, they can set their own high standards and get things done.

Here, as in every part of democratic life, the question is one of balance: autonomy and control, freedom and equality. Responsibility for the 9–4 of *schooling* is shared currently between government and professionals, acting on behalf of the electorate, but responsibility for *education* is shared more widely. In truth, education is not, as those promoting marketisation reforms argue, a 'service' delivered to 'consumers', nor is any one authority solely responsible. Aligning schooling with education has limited our understanding and consequent capacity for real improvement. Schooling is only one part of lifelong personal development, an individual journey whose start is jointly constructed by parent, child, community and school. Those advocating a performance culture associated with targets and nationally agreed 'performance criteria', disempower those within the school community. It is much harder for school education to be 'co-constructed' by professionals, children, parents and community, when national targets dominate the agenda, and the professional community answers to those in superior positions in the bureaucratic and political hierarchy of power. The Common Weal report on 'Children and Young People' argues for a culture of participation, not top-down performance. In our schooling system, that has to start in the school community, not with elected politicians.

> **Issue #6:** Government should initiate discussions on reforms in school governance to empower further local school communities while also retaining strategic capacity and high quality professional networks. The process should not be 'political' (horse-trading by different vested interests), but educational (what will produce the best educational outcome for children).

Teachers' changing responsibilities

Teachers' work has changed substantially since I entered the profession. In this they are no different to many other workers in today's restless globalised economy. One thing is not in doubt – it has never been more important to have well qualified motivated teachers in our schools. This is borne out by the Finnish experience where all teachers have a Masters degree, enjoy a substantial amount of professional autonomy and rank in status alongside doctors and lawyers:

> Since Finland emerged in 2000 as the top-scoring (**OECD**) nation on PISA, researchers have been pouring into the country to study the so-called 'Finnish miracle'. How did a country with an undistinguished education system in the 1980s surge to the head of the global class ... one element ... trumps all others: excellent teachers and leaders.[38]

Curriculum policy makers may write things on bits of paper but we need teachers who can make sense of them for the children in each classroom. Within the very different structures of the primary and secondary school, the teacher is the 'mediator' of the curriculum to particular individuals and groups, adjusting content and expectations to create the best interface between the talents, motivations and capabilities of the child and the demands of the curriculum. The role of teachers is no longer just teaching, but helping all children to learn. This remains the biggest challenge of the school teacher – to help every child gain access to the powerful life-enhancing knowledge and experience of the curriculum, to the 'best that humanity has thought, said and done'[39] by knowing the child, the curriculum and the best ways to bring them together for each child.

For some pupils, learning from books, in words and numbers, comes easily and may even take place independently of the teacher. For others, as illustrated above, the impact of the learning environment the teacher creates in the classroom can be powerfully positive or negative in shaping their learning experience. This relational aspect of the school experience can be as important as the more impersonal work of the curriculum. Up to age 11, the absence of high-stakes competitive testing gives the primary and early years teacher room to respond to the children as individuals. In secondary schools, it can be more difficult to resist the dominance of the examination curriculum – pupils can come to see themselves as being more important to the teacher and the school for *how they perform* rather than for *who they are*. The functional requirements of the curriculum and the 50 minute classroom may leave little space for personal attention – content must be covered – quadratic equations or alternating current or the causes of World War 1 – before moving on to the next part of the syllabus. Some would argue this shift, to a more impersonal, less supported, more task-focussed way is part of growing up – but this underestimates the extent to which a teenage pupil is still a child.

Good teachers establish a positive climate by their enthusiasm and drive, by their organisation, by their awareness of their pupils as people. A teacher's every action is loaded with meaning – even something as apparently straightforward as how a teacher hands back a test. One says '25 others in the class did better than you.' Another smiles and says 'some things to learn here – I've noted them and we can work on them together, but I really liked this answer because …' The same piece of work, different messages. Maintaining the balance between respectful personal relationships that generate trust and the curricular requirements that drive the work is one of the unsung skills of the good teacher. A judicious mix of care and challenge is all the more needed with the wider social inclusion agenda of ASL and GIRFEC, particularly in schools where there are larger numbers of children with social, emotional or behavioural problems.

Teachers are now challenged to be more expert in a range of areas: academic knowledge in literacy, numeracy and other subject areas; knowledge about learning; new technical skills in teaching from co-operative learning to smartboards, social inclusion, development delays, health and well-being (under Curriculum for Excellence a responsibility of all teachers). Above all, they are required to have a human touch. For many teachers the most challenging work, because of its emotional immediacy, involves dealing with difficult behaviour, a much bigger issue in some schools than others. In the old-style disciplinary system of the past, punishment-based control shut the issue down: children were held responsible for their behaviour and punishment/reward systems were designed to train them. Detentions, punishment exercises and so on still operate in many schools, but 'inclusion' demands that schools and teachers work through relationships. Like medical professionals in Accident and Emergency, teachers are sometimes in the front line for abusive, emotionally charged behaviour but the child does not go away when the emergency is over. The teacher still has to get the best from that child the next day, and the day after.

The mobile phone incident of the previous chapter is typical of how classroom incidents can flare up and take over, but also of how complex the back-story can be. Getting at the underlying issues can be difficult and time consuming. 'Restorative practice', for example, involves one-to-one conversations, or time-costly restorative meetings. While these meetings go on, are other pupils getting less attention? Some teachers and pupils may want a violent or abusive child to 'go away' by being excluded so others can get on with their work, but we know that exclusion is often worse for the child, and in the long run for the community. It is not easy to find the right balance between holding up the standards of behaviour expected in a public space while motivating and maintaining trust, even with those disrupting the work of others. This is the kind of behind-the-scenes work of today's teachers which makes the job very different to what was expected twenty or thirty years ago.

The 2010 report *Teaching Scotland's Future* proposed a number of generally well-received changes to how teachers are trained initially and developed in post. National working groups, teacher organisations, universities and local authorities are working together to deliver on these proposals. The report fell short of recommending that Scottish teachers, like those in Finland, should all be qualified to Masters degree level, but this can surely only be a question of time. Many other professions require a Masters degree qualification. In teaching, where the first degree studies of teachers are so diverse, the greater depth of Masters degree programmes would help develop the common language and common professional values to which the new teacher 'standards' aim. All of this raises a vitally important question: how much is Scotland willing to pay for a teaching profession qualified to the best international standards?

School leaders

In the 1980s, the model of school leadership favoured by Scottish local authorities was of an efficient middle manager, implementing council policies and meeting inspectorate requirements. [40] As a headteacher in the 90s, reading research and analytical texts from other countries, I felt that in Scotland we needed a better 'story' about what school leaders did. When I was appointed as headteacher at Crieff in the early 90s, preparation for school headship was uneven, *ad hoc* and some of the demands of the post were perplexing. That was one of the reasons I went to work at Edinburgh University in 2000 to introduce the new Scottish Qualification for Headship (**SQH**). Since 2000, SQH has prepared the current generation of school leaders more consistently. In the late 1980s, it was rare to find any school leader who had read recent research. Now it is rare to find one who has not. Alongside the qualification was a new 'Standard for Headship', making clear the complexity of the headteacher's job, the politics of the job, the educational values at its heart. The qualification is currently being updated to fit better with the world of Curriculum for Excellence and the new 'Standard for Leadership'.

School leaders play a vital role in the quality of schooling. It is, however, easy to overemphasise the 'leadership effect' when power and influence are so widely distributed in the Scottish system. Leadership is not just found in the head-teacher, but throughout a school community. The 2010 report, 'Teaching Scotland's Future', on which current teacher training reforms are based, reads as if schools exist in a social vacuum and that the quality of children's education is entirely down to teachers and school leaders. It assumes that with the silver bullets of better teaching and better leader-ship, Scotland's educational problems will be sorted. School leaders, burdened with this expectation, can easily take on too much, feeling that they alone should sort all the problems that face their pupils, then buckling under stressful over-work. Peter Gronn coined the term 'greedy work' to capture the increasing demands of the role. He writes: 'Greedy work is such that it demands that one be ... always attentive, alert, absorbed in and utterly committed to the particular task as a totally functioning, fully available, non-stop cognitive and emotional presence in the workplace ...'[41]

More recently Gronn was involved with a research team which conducted a detailed study into the recruitment and retention of headteachers in Scotland, a problem for some local authorities. While they found that the work of Scottish headteachers has all the characteristics of 'greedy work', they also found that the vast majority loved the educational part of their job. The biggest source of dissatisfaction was not workload, but restrictions on professional freedom. Head-teachers said lack of 'autonomy' (that word again) was a major negative feature of their work, making the inevitable dilemmas of their work more frequent and more difficult. I speak from experience when I say that Millar and Hall in an earlier book in the 'Postcards' series, *Letting Go,* could have used the work of headteachers as a perfect example of the 'organisational disease' of over-regulation. The restrictions on professional autonomy identified by the research into headteacher recruitment included a lack of power over budgets and staffing and 'the need to address frequent requests from local authorities and other organisations', rather than spend their time with the children and teachers.[42]

Perhaps our school leaders have too many responsibilities, particularly those who work in authorities which never fully implemented the intention of the 2001 teachers' agreement that business managers should take over the financial and organisational routines of school. Should there be further experiments with different ways to manage and lead a school organisation? Here, as elsewhere, our current governance arrangements restrict experimentation. The same professional and bureaucratic management hierarchies, negotiated nationally between employers, government and teacher associations, are found in every Scottish school. In some other countries and systems, teachers in a school collectively agree the best way of rewarding their work within the available budget and to match the school's priorities, with the school leader chosen by staff, parents and pupils for a five year period of office with the possibility of 'recall' where required.

Who is accountable?

Like responsibility, accountability for schooling is a confused complicated business, as illustrated in the example below of what happened to Ronnie. At the political level, division of responsibility can lead to confused accountability. Neither national nor local government is responsible for every aspect of schooling, so each can deflect accountability by blaming the other – local authorities can point to inadequately funded or unworkable policy, and national government to inefficient delivery. Both can blame teachers or headteachers for 'not implementing policy properly'. Within local authorities, senior officials experience tension between corporate internal priorities and educational outcomes. I have often found that, as in any big organisation, local authority officials can find it hard to prioritise their accountability towards those in a school community, since their primary accountability is to their bosses within the corporate hierarchy. They may also lack operational experience of the sectors they manage. Someone with an early years background will struggle to understand the issues facing a secondary headteacher and vice versa. Without accurate diagnosis of the problem based on expert knowledge, supportive targeted intervention is replaced by general assertions, or worse, bullying demands. Finding a scapegoat may answer a short-term need for someone to be accountable, but seldom addresses the underlying problem.

As a headteacher, I always felt my most important accountability was directly, face to face, to the parents, pupils and staff of the school community – two-way exchanges through which trust is built and a common 'story' of the school develops. Teachers often speak in the same way about 'putting their pupils first'. However my primary contractual accountability, and that of the teachers, was to the Council, my employer. Top-down demands and bottom-up needs often met on the headteacher's desk.

Who *should be* accountable and to whom?

Teachers and headteachers are rightly in the front line of accountability for how our school system works. Councils supposedly quality assure the work of schools, typically following the templates of HMIE, whose incomplete analysis was highlighted above. Scottish headteachers have more limited powers over teachers than their English or private sector counterparts, but both teachers and heads are accountable to their employer through personnel policies of discipline, competence, capability and absence management and to their professional body for their professional standards and for keeping themselves up to date. Scottish Councils, as employers, are in my experience generally very supportive of teachers as employees. Supported by strong and effective professional associations, teachers enjoy tolerant conditions of service which are the envy of many in less favoured jobs. Teachers have very individual qualities, so beyond the basic minimum standard there can be great variety in what they contribute to the broader life of the school as well as their own classroom: schools need a balance of personalities and talents.

The paperwork and expectations of the many new national policies and local authority guidelines of Curriculum for Excellence, GIRFEC and so on, are each worthy in their own right, striving to improve school education and teacher practice by detailed regulation. However despite the excellent conditions of service which they enjoy, many teachers feel under a disempowering and demotivating top-down weight from these policies and the paperwork that goes with them. When teachers begin to feel that they are just functionaries, carrying out someone else's instructions, they can lose the gleam in the eye that awakens the enthusiasm of their pupils. There is an opportunity cost involved in every extra standardised procedure – less opportunity for the teacher to bring their own enthusiasms to the job, directly to their pupils. This is even more the case for school leaders, at the centre of a whirlwind of pressures and expectations from above and below. In the past, individual teachers had more space and time to be creative, take risks, in a specific place, with a specific group of children, but too much freedom leaves inadequate teaching practice unchallenged. Finding the balance between helpful standardisation and creative autonomy is one of the key challenges for policy. Although one of the main aims of Curriculum for Excellence was to find just such a new balance, recent surveys suggest that many have experienced it thus far as an imposition rather than liberation.

At all levels of democratic life, the tension between autonomy and control can be highly creative. Miller and Hall, in *Letting Go*, illustrate how such tension can cause problems within organisations if badly handled. Under-regulated work, including teaching, where each organisation or worker decides what an acceptable standard should be, can, at its worst, lead to toleration of poor performance and malpractice, even within the so-called caring professions. This was evident in the 2013 report of the work of midStaffordshire NHS Trust. There has to be accountability, but intelligent accountability recognises the interaction of different levels of responsibility. The current hierarchical mechanistic accountability of the 'official' account is overly simplistic and responsibility and accountability are thus sometimes misaligned. The present accountability model, with professional inspectors judging the quality of school education on behalf of the civic community, cannot help us improve much further. The school community should assume a stronger role in accountability and should have access to, but not be controlled by, consultancy expertise and quality data.

Issue #7: Scotland should move towards a system where the accountability of a school is evenly weighted between national and local authority expectations and the views of the parents and pupils of the school community, whose individual voices are given more weight through regular opportunities for structured direct feedback.

Confused Accountability

Ronnie was going through a hard time a couple of years into his post as headteacher. The previous head was not known for innovation or educational thinking and Ronnie was full of energy and ambition to move the school forward, but he faced great challenges. The school he was working in was in an area with many social problems. Among many other incidents, Ronnie had been physically threatened by local drug dealers when trying to make the school grounds into a safe area. A number of his promoted staff, in their 50s, had been appointed to their posts in the early 1980s and 'had seen it all before'. They were not willing to engage with the new 'inclusive' agenda in school which he wanted to promote. As he saw it, they had 'dug themselves into trenches and they're not for coming out'. For them, school was a battleground and they were not going to give up the tools they used to retain their position. His influential school staff representative was also a staff association representative on the Joint Negotiating Committee of the Council and therefore a significant player in council circles. This man made it very difficult for Ronnie to introduce any new ideas into the school, or if they were introduced, sabotaged them covertly through his influence in the staffroom.

Ronnie felt that he needed support to 'take on' this influence in the school. He approached the then Director with a proposal to discipline the member of staff for failure to follow instructions, as it was the only way he could assert his authority as headteacher and thus reduce the other's influence, but was advised not to do so. It was, he was told, 'not a case you can win.' This was one of a number of ways in which he felt his hands had been tied in his new post. In sounding off to me, he talked about resigning, but carried on and made, he felt, a little progress. The biannual local authority Quality Improvement Officer's (**QIO**) report on Ronnie's school judged it as satisfactory. Three years later, inspectors visited the school for the first time since Ronnie's appointment and reported that the school was 'weak' in several respects, as Ronnie knew only too well.

The Council pushed Ronnie into an unwelcome early retirement with no financial settlement. The new headteacher was given the support Ronnie had asked for to make the necessary changes, including generous pay-offs for the early retirement of some key personnel. The Director, who had both supported Ronnie's appointment and shaped the parameters of his leadership, and the QIO whose judgement on the school was now deemed to be poor, carried on in post. Ronnie had some of the responsibility but was landed with all of the accountability. Should others have been accountable?

CHAPTER FIVE
A new alignment of school and community

Futurologists predict that pupils in our schools today face a daunting future: overpopulation and resource wars, followed by global warming and environmental catastrophe, accompanied by ironic observations that all predictions are unpredictable. Regular scare stories trumpet growing risks from poor diet, obesity, and an unsafe internet. It's even risky to have had risk-averse parents who protected you too much. It is commonly claimed that those currently in school will be worse off than their parents, with massive debts accumulated while at university, less job security and the prospect of a much longer working life. What's more they are at the mercy of social forces they can't control, such as the banking collapse and the all-powerful globalising market. Meanwhile the spendthrift baby boomers, having used up the wealth that could have built a better future, will demand more resources to meet the care needs of their lengthy retirement. Despite these dodgy predictions, which, together with continuing patterns of social inequality can be spun into a negative future spiral, I am optimistic. Schools are reservoirs of stability and hope in a changing world. The enthusiasm of the young constantly re-energises their teachers. Scottish primary schools in particular are widely recognised as out-standing. The 2007 OECD report observed:

> The greatest strength of Scottish education is its primary schools. They educate all children in common – including most of those with special needs – and are thus exposed to the full range of the population. . . . that primary schools are responding so well to the challenge {of building a solid platform for all children} ... would justify significant increased investment in them . . . targeted to where the challenge is most acute.[43]

In secondary education, whence children move into our unequal adult society, the inequity of the Scottish system becomes most evident and current systems and structures are under most pressure, yet here too, optimism is a justified reaction to the vibrant enthusiastic learning environments in many of our schools. Scottish schools have improved greatly since I entered the profession – more inclusive, more supportive, and with higher levels of achievement and a broader vision of what school education can be and should do. There have always been great teachers in our schools, naturals with knowledge and enthusiasm aplenty, but in general teachers and headteachers are now better-informed and better trained within a better regulated profession. All around Scotland new and refurbished buildings and grounds have acquired better facilities, while constant rapid change in the use of computers, tablets and the internet opens up new learning options. Using current performance measures, more Scottish pupils than ever before are included and supported and attain higher standards in national examinations. In my current work with senior school leaders at the University of Edinburgh I find inspiration and enthusiasm at every turn. I also found inspiration and optimism aplenty in my school tour recorded in my online journal: the young committee members who run their own artistic studio in Room 13 of Caol Primary; the environmentalists of Bucksburn H.S., sharing with their peers in Sweden and with the business community of Aberdeen their vision of a more sustainable future; the young people of Auchenharvie, passionate in their pride in their school and their community; the caring attitudes of the senior pupils of St John's Academy Perth towards the young pupils who share the campus.

Despite these many positives, there is plenty of room for improvement. The statistics tell us that a substantial number of pupils, including many from the least affluent groups in society, continue to fall through the net each year into the same low-skilled insecure future as their parents. The wider aims of Curriculum for Excellence, encapsulated in the 'four capacities', are neither measured nor to some extent measureable, nor can we tell whether the curriculum structures of Curriculum for Excellence will deliver these capacities. The hidden curriculum continues to value some pupils more than others particularly at the senior phase. There is, moreover, some doubt as to whether the current schooling system, with its conservative bias towards stability, is sufficiently flexible or diverse to take advantage of the opportunities for flexible learning offered by the rapidly developing knowledge environment. The book began by asking, 'Can today's schooling system provide the best education for all children growing up in Scotland, now and in the future?' Despite many improvements and my optimism for the future, the overall evidence of the book suggests the answer is 'no', leading inevitably to the second question, 'if not, what should be done to improve the schooling system?'

Over the past fifty years, schooling has evolved within the umbrella of the model set out in 1965. The vision behind that model was that comprehensive, child-centred schooling would give all children an equal start in life, while maintaining the standards of the selective system it replaced. This would be achieved in schools staffed by professional teachers, run by local authorities, within a framework set by national government. Subsequent reforms, from Standard Grade through 5–14 to ASL and Curriculum for Excellence, all fit within this broad vision – seeking a balance between top-down authority (both the curriculum of human knowledge and the political hierarchies of state power) and the bottom-up reality of the child's experience (outside of school, in family and locality). This model of schooling as a constantly improving professional 'service' has delivered steady progress but is nearing the end of its course. Schooling is only a part of education; teachers can only teach so much. Curriculum for Excellence in its present form has left the job unfinished. The current improvement model, based on demanding more and more of the school and its teachers, cannot bring all the change needed. *Schooling needs to be reconfigured as part of a wider educational project in which all Scotland needs to play a part.*

If we want children to learn to live better in community we need to create communities of learning where they *actually do* live better. This is not about measurement and outcomes, but about quality of experience. The current schooling system, particularly secondary, builds in, for some, alienation, inequity and division. Despite the many personal relationships of care and affection within a school, at its end point the system ranks children formally on only one measure of what it means to be a fully flourishing human being, and anticipation of this ranking feeds its way back through the system, in parental memory and in the anticipation of current pupils. Current hierarchical management structures and complicated professional routines exaggerate distances between home and school. For some in our society this is schooling by regulation (*done to*) rather than schooling by participation (*done with and for*). Moreover, as argued in Chapter Four, this model encourages people to think in the wrong ways about responsibility and accountability. Where professional teachers either have too much loaded on them by their employers or load too many expectations on themselves, the child, the parent, the community can be left out, or kept out, of their part in the educational process. We need to realign the contributions of all those involved in educational processes, so that they work better together.

To some extent these questions are political, not just educational. Advocates of different options have different views about the best balance between individual freedoms and state control. At one end of the spectrum is the free for all of the English system, with elite public schools, academies, free schools and local authority comprehensive schools competing for their pupils, at the other the egalitarian Finnish comprehensive model. Scotland's managed uniformity, with state schools sitting alongside a thriving private sector, lies somewhere in between. Deciding on the right balance point in schooling, between a freer system and one which aims to provide an even playing field through positive interventions, is a political and moral issue, not one that can be answered 'objectively.' My proposed model is therefore inevitably both political and educational. A more socially focussed, less individualistically competitive model of education has the potential to deliver better educational experiences for all, even those advantaged by the current system, but can only come at the expense of some individual freedoms and some additional state and community controls. Any vision for schooling has to be a vision also for the society beyond. Mine fits with a recent Social Europe paper in which Henning Meyer proposes a 'good society' based on democracy, community and pluralism where social goods of inclusion, education and health take precedence over market interests and individualistic consumerism.[44]

The aphorism, 'It takes all Scotland to raise a child', sums up the philosophy underpinning this book. We need a system that allows our professionals, politicians, parents and local communities to pull together better behind the education of our children. The structure of early years, followed by 5–12 (not 4½–12!) and 12–18 comprehensive neighbourhood schools, operating ASL, GIRFEC and Curriculum for Excellence, anchors our system. We now need a new relationship of school and community if it is to work at its best. The primary responsibility for bringing up a child lies with the parent or carer. But at every stage the community, the school and the state are already there, influencing and constraining the possibilities for the child: their actions and systems can work for or against particular children and families, in particular contexts, often in unintended ways. Through better understanding of the respective influences, we can find a better balance between the forces of liberty and equality, autonomy and control, bottom-up and top-down. In schooling in particular, this means supporting schools and teachers as they strive to mediate between the powerful knowledge of the curriculum and the life of the child. The two ways through which I propose that this realignment of schooling and education, school and community, can be made to work in practice are through the evolutionary redevelopment of schools into networks of community learning hubs and through the introduction of a challenging Scottish Graduation Certificate, primary and secondary, accessible to all young people when leaving primary school and again at age 18.

The school community learning hub

In the schooling system I envisage, primary and secondary schools remain as strong identifiable institutions. However, rather than providing all of a child's learning opportunities, the school over time changes into a learning hub, networked with other school learning hubs to support the kinds of desirable professional collaboration raised as Issue #2 above. There is teaching as we know it at the core, particularly during the 'broad general education' of Curriculum for Excellence and in the demanding disciplinary work that prepares pupils for Highers and Advanced Highers. Schools continue to mentor and support pupils, even those in the later stages who may be receiving most of their education elsewhere. Young people enjoy working with and learning from adults other than teachers in contexts other than school. Much of the applied learning of the classroom can also benefit the community. Where this happens, as in the examples highlighted in my school tour, it brings great benefits to school and community, but at present it is episodic. From helping plant community orchards to volunteer visiting in a care home, from 'garden-busting' to litter picking, from dog-walking to entertaining, harnessing the talent and enthusiasm of young people in a structured systematic way has great potential to enrich our community life, while relationships with older people have much to contribute to the young.

In the community learning hub, pupils share community activities, learn in classrooms and library, but may also learn in other community locations, use informal and online learning and learn through community service, work experience, in co-operative and intergenerational activities. In such centres, people of all ages will work together to enquire, to develop their knowledge and understanding, to learn from each other and work with each other to answer the difficult questions they face in their lives and their civic choices. The support some young people need will come not just from professional services but from closer relationships within the community, suitably structured and quality assured. In community learning hubs, school pupils can break out of the age-segregated insularities of school society and work across the generations. These are spaces where community and learning are reborn, spaces for empowering dialogues across the generations.

This model is already in place in some of our primary schools and early years (pre-five) establishments, freed from the constraints of tight examination syllabi to develop strong connections to parents and to the surrounding community. In my school tour there was plenty of evidence of school and community living and working together in Wee Pans, in the beautifully designed St Bernadettes in Larbert and in the new community learning campus in Caol, due to open in 2016. Aspects of the model are also in place in some of our secondary schools, particularly those with well-developed networks and strong social capital such as Bucksburn, or where, as in parts of Perth and Kinross and in Fife's proposed new Levenmouth campus, the local authority has worked to deliver a broad strategic vision of community education. These are not new ideas, but they need the support of a consistent long-term national vision if they are to flourish everywhere.

Catchment area and transport are important factors in developing a sense of community around local school learning hubs. In his book imagining a different future, *Schooling When The Oil Runs Out* (2011), Michael Bassey points out the unsustainability of wasteful current practices of school transport, clogging urban streets during the school run hours. Children should spend less time in cars and buses and more time in activity. The internet and smartphones, however fast and cleverly they develop, complement face-to-face contact – they can never substitute for it. It is that face to face character of school communities that is their strongest feature, through which learning to live in community takes place. Housing and community planning should ensure that over the long run, every Scottish urban child, and every rural child where possible, can walk or cycle safely to a local school, bringing locality and schooling back together, and that school catchment areas, within collaborative school networks, should as far as possible represent the diversity of relative poverty and affluence, allowing Scottish children to experience and learn from the social diversity of Scotland as a whole. Planning criteria for all housing developments should include the contribution the development will make to the social diversity of the neighbouring schools.

> **Issue #8:** Government should, over time, support the evolution of schools into networks of socially diverse local community learning hubs.

To encourage school networks and community organisations into structured collaborative planning to benefit young people, I propose that Scotland develops a high stakes graduation certificate.

The Scottish Graduation Certificate

The graduation certificate I envisage would be awarded at the end of both primary and secondary. It requires the whole community to play its part in educating our children and provides a structure for that to happen. In primary, it builds on work already done on profiling the talents of pupils at P7. National certification will ensure consistent priority for the broader aims of Curriculum for Excellence, already embedded in many primary schools, and give value to wider community-based activities in which many primary schools excel. Graduating from primary school with a national certificate, each child has his or her unique talents and achievements recognised, together with the learning skills they take to secondary school.

In secondary there is more work to be done. The academic progression from Scotland's schools to her universities and colleges is secure, respected and well understood in the community, but wide-ranging concern about routes of progression directly into work, or into workplace preparation, despite all the work that has gone into Curriculum for Excellence, is reflected in the many recent turbulent developments in the post-16 sector. Angela Constance was given Cabinet Secretary responsibility for 'Training, Youth and Women's Employment', a sign of the importance SG attaches to this area of its work. Skills Development Scotland has been shaking up the national framework for careers. The governance of colleges has been reformed, with mergers creating new 'super-colleges'. The Wood Commission has published its final report into 'Developing Scotland's Young Workforce' (2014), making clear continuing widespread dissatisfaction with current arrangements. One of the difficulties is that these developments, and the debates associated with them, take place in a different bubble from those affecting schools. Most parents know little of developments in this sector. Few teachers or local authority officials understand the complex changing map of post-school progression outwith the straightforward Higher to university route which they followed themselves.

The current examination system drives so much practice in secondary school because it is the *only* national high-stakes process through which school work is valued. The national debate of 2002, the subsequent initial Curriculum for Excellence report of 2004, the 2007 OECD report and all the current activity in this area makes clear that Scotland needs to see vocational and academic learning brought together for all, Scotland-wide, not just in pockets of excellence. The proposed 'senior phase' of Curriculum for Excellence is permissive and weak. It needs to be reinforced by a stronger, more easily understood national system of graduation certification.

Scotland should follow England's lead and require all young people to be in compulsory education of some form or another through to graduation at age 18. Pathways to graduation will be diverse: almost completely in school (with only short programmes outwith for example through work experience and community service); part-school/part work-training; part school/part voluntary or community service; part school/part college; or any combination – but should be clear enough to allow resources and people to gather round in support. Scotland's secondary schools, and the young people within them, need the framework of a Scottish graduation certificate that reflects the values of our schooling system, open to all young people, inclusive not exclusive. In secondary it would also join up the senior phase with the outcomes of current discussions based on the Wood Commission report.[45] Local authorities, employers, third sector and community organisations and schools will require to collaborate in order to fill out the graduation framework with detailed programmes.

The graduation concept also creates a point around which every child's achievement can be celebrated in graduation ceremonies. In the inclusive school communities of the future, all our pupils should be able to graduate at age 18, as a formal rite of passage, a recognition of what they have achieved in school and of their progress into the more adult world beyond; a process which balances the top-down framing of the curriculum with the natural or intrinsic talents of the young person.

What would a Scottish child have to do to graduate? We already have a robust model in programmes such as the Duke of Edinburgh Award, where candidates have to attain a standard in a number of broad categories, with flexible options within each category. It would not be either/or, separating academic

Figure B: A possible Scottish Secondary Graduation Certificate (*all elements to be completed*)

Category	Examples of qualifying activities	Notes
Learning pathway	Different blends of school, college, work, voluntary and community activity and learning within the different pathways, some leading to employment at age 18, some to College and some to University.	This section sets out the individual's broad post-school pathway in accordance with Wood Commission recommendations.
Academic progress	Core literacy and numeracy National courses taken Other courses or awards	Compulsory (with support for those with additional support needs). A record of courses taken and passed or gained. Maths Challenge, Young Scientist etc.
Community service	Voluntary Service Participation in community enterprise and activity of various kinds Sub-elements of other awards (e.g. Duke of Edinburgh Award, John Muir Award, ASDAN...) or through Scouts, Cadets etc. Young carers	A progression across the secondary years can be shown.

Category	Examples of qualifying activities	Notes
Skills	For example, in music, the arts, craft, horticulture, animal husbandry, technical skills, information technology skills	Practical / performance focus: a very flexible element similar to Duke of Edinburgh allowing graduates to showcase any special skills
Working life	Work experience (paid or unpaid) Employability award Interpersonal skills, communication skills, teamwork, leadership	Emphasis on practical experience and practical skills. Employer reference part of the 'work experience' element.
Challenging experience	Examples: Expedition, residential sponsored activity, enterprise	Flexible options to incorporate a range of activities which were taken on in the 'senior phase' and which were new and challenging for the individual
Personal assessment	An 'end of school' personal review of Achievements, growth and challenges to come. Health and wellbeing.	Development for the 'personal statement' of the current University Entry process.

and vocational routes, but both recognising the value of different types of learning experience and achievement. The certificate should be sufficiently challenging that it requires effort and commitment, sufficiently flexible that it can reflect the diversity of individual talent and sufficiently structured to reflect the breadth of outcomes and experiences at which Curriculum for Excellence aims. The certificate should be created *with* the pupil, not something done *to* them. Figure B is a starter for discussion. Whether a young person is still attending school, or receiving their education in another location, the collation and certification of graduation entitlement and associated administrative functions should still be the responsibility of the school, acting as a co-ordinating hub for the different parts of the system and ensuring continuity of support for the pupils.

There should be no grading in the Scottish Graduation Certificate. Elements of the certificate (e.g. examinations, or Duke of Edinburgh Awards), may be graded for their own specific purposes, but it is important that the entire certificate gives a clear message that every worthwhile route into the adult world at 18 has *equal value*. Self assessment should be part of the process. All those with additional support needs of various kinds should be able to achieve an individual route to graduation, appropriately supported, included with equal value in a new community celebration of what they have achieved during their time in school.

> **Issue #9:** to structure and improve the educational relationship between schooling and community, and ensure greater equity in our schooling system, Government should develop a challenging Scottish Graduation Certificate, achievable by all.

Conclusion

What has been proposed in this book is not an action plan, crossing every 't' and dotting every 'i', with a clear time frame and appropriate resourcing. It identifies system changes which together can realign schooling, education and community to deliver a strong, fairer education for all Scotland's children. Over time, relevant officers and professionals, working with and for elected authorities, can take advantage of opportunities that arise to respond to the different issues raised above. Evolutionary change is usually best. Community learning hubs, often with other support services on site, can already be found in embryonic form in many parts of Scotland, while joint campus schools bringing primary and secondary, mainstream and special or catholic and secular together can be found in all parts of the country. However in some places, local authorities have signed 30-year leasing deals on particular types of school and change will follow a different arc.

At several points above I have asked 'what is Scotland willing to pay?', yet in this year of the independence debate we are constantly reminded that Scotland is a rich country. Budgets are tight now, but perhaps new taxes hypothecated for beneficial educational developments might release more cash. Even with more money, room for experiment is limited. Not all change can take place at one time. It is always desirable for the early stages of new development to be carried out by enthusiasts who have the energy and commitment to work through the inevitable teething problems.

The challenge for government is to establish an educational framework which liberates the creativity and enthusiasm of all children and challenges them to develop their learning skills and disciplined knowledge as a basis for future learning, while at the same time reducing the potentially damaging impact of wider social factors on the life chances of some children. That demands intervention, not laissez-faire, but an intervention that respects the family and community. If forced, it can damage what it is designed to support. Primary schools, often smaller, physically closer to the local community, and nurturing, balance this well for younger children. Secondary, progressing children towards different pathways into the adult world, and delivering more demanding subject-based learning, must find a different balance. In both contexts, the challenge for teachers, for schools and for the schooling system is to find the best balance for each child.

Each and every one of the issues I have raised can contribute to the evolution of a stronger, fairer system of schooling, within a broader concept of education as a collaborative activity in which all Scotland plays its part in supporting the education of all Scotland's children. To recap:

- no child should start school before age 5 (issue #1 page 22)

- public and private schools should work together in local professional networks, sharing resources and responsibilities for aspects of the school experience of all local children (issue #2 page 36)

- every child should have free stimulating outwith-classroom learning experiences (issue #3 page 56)

- parents, pupils and staff should have a stronger voice in evaluating their school experience (issue #4 page 60)

- rigorous confidential standardised assessments in literacy and numeracy, and parallel reviews of health and well-being, should contribute to annual collaborative home-school planning of a child's development (issue #5 page 63)

- parents and the school community should have a stronger role in governance, reducing the role of top-down inspection, but with elected authorities with sufficient capacity providing strategic oversight and resourcing (issues #6 and #7 pages 93 and 103)

- Government should, over time, support the evolution of schools into networks of socially diverse local community learning hubs (issue #8 page 115)

- to structure and improve the educational relationship between schooling and community, and ensure greater equity in our schooling system, Government should develop a challenging Scottish Graduation Certificate, achievable by all (issue #9 page 120)

As with the schooling developments of the past fifty years, there will be many evolutionary adjustments along the way – some trial, some error. But Scotland requires a public schooling system supported by the whole nation, one which gathers its resources and its support around *every* child, the children of Ian as well as Jim, Elaine as well as Catherine – a system in which schooling plays its important part in delivering a broader and fairer education.

In the 21st century it will take all Scotland to raise all Scotland's children.

Notes

Additional source references can be found online by using the link on the book's homepage at http://www.postcardsfromscotland.co.uk/book_07.html

1   See Craig, C. (2011) *The Great Takeover*, Glendaruel: Argyll Publishing.
2   http://www.postcardsfromscotland.co.uk/book_07.html
3   Wedge, P. and Prosser, H. (1973) *Born to Fail*, London: Arrow Books (for National Children's Bureau), p. 6.
4   OECD (2007*) Quality and Equity of Schooling in Scotland*, Paris, OECD p. 68.
5   I am grateful to Dr Bill Maxwell of Education Scotland for this chart, distilled from national data.
6   Macmillan, L., Tyler, C. and Vignoles, A. (2013) *Who gets the top jobs? The role of family background and networks in recent graduates' access to high status professions* DoQSS Workings Paper No.13–15, Institute of Education, University of London.
7   Statistics available at http://www.scotland.gov.uk/ Publications/2013/06/7503/downloads, accessed 08.03.14.
8   Wilby, P. (2013) *Britain's qualification spiral is beginning to unravel*, *The Guardian* 8.1.13, available at http://www.theguardian.com/commentisfree/2013/jan/08/q ualification-spiral-is-unravelling accessed 8.8.14
9   Ianell, C. (2011) Educational Expansion and Social Mobility, *Social Policy and Society,* 10:2, p. 251.

10 Hoskins, K. and Barker, B. (2014) *Dreams of Success,* London: Trentham/Institute of Education

11 Quoted in Heath, A. and Sullivan, A. (2011), 'The democratisation of upper secondary education?', *Oxford Review of Education*, 37:2, p. 136.

12 Wilkinson, R. and Pickett, K. (2010) *The Spirit Level*, London: Allen Lane, p. 10.

13 http://www.pnas.org/content/107/38/16489.full accessed 15.05.14

14 Marmot, M. (2004) *The Status Syndrome: How your social standing directly affects your health and life expectancy*, London: Bloomsbury; Burns, H. (2014) 'What causes health?' *Journal of the Royal College of Physicians of Edinburgh*, 44: pp. 103–5.

15 Hirsch, D. (2014) *The cost of a child in 2014,* London: Child Poverty Action Group; see also the Daily Record report: *Soaring childcare costs and benefit cuts are condemning struggling families to life of poverty, study reveals* @ http://www.dailyrecord.co.uk/news/scottish-news/soaring-childcare-costs-benefit-cuts-4038243, accessed 12.8.14.

16 See, for example, UNESCO 'Education for All' @ http://www.unesco.org/new/en/education/themes/leading-the-international-agenda/education-for-all/, accessed 13.08.14.

17 OECD (2007) *Quality and Equity of Schooling in Scotland.* Paris: OECD.

18 See, for example, http://www.ofsted.gov.uk/resources/london-challenge, accessed 13.08.14.

19 GUS @ http://growingupinscotland.org.uk/,The Guardian (2014) *Free tuition in Scotland benefits wealthiest students the most* @ http://www.theguardian.com/education/2014/ apr/29/free-tuition-scotland-benefits-wealthiest-students-most-study, accessed 13.08.14.

20 See http://seasonsforgrowth.co.uk/, accessed 13.08.14.

21 Scottish Executive, *A Curriculum for Excellence* @

http://www.scotland.gov.uk/Publications/2004/11/20178/45862, accessed 13.08.14.

22 McIlroy, C. (2013) Chapter 41, 'The Scottish Approach to School Improvement: achievements and limitations' pp. 434–445 in Bryce, T. Humes, W. Gillies, D. and Kennedy, A. eds, *Scottish Education*, Edinburgh University Press (4th Edition).

23 Donaldson, G. (2009) *Improving Scottish Education* @ http://www.educationscotland.gov.uk/Images/ise09_tcm4-712882.pdf, accessed 13.08.14.

24 Stoll, L. (1999) 'Realising Our Potential: Understanding and Developing Capacity for Lasting Improvement', *School Effectiveness and School Improvement*, vol.10, no.4, pp. 503–532.

25 Hoskins, K. and Barker, B. (2014) *Dreams of Success, op.cit.*

26 Dahl, R. (1982) *Dilemmas of Pluralist Democracy – Autonomy vs. Control.* New Haven and London: Yale University Press.

27 Crick, B., (1978) 'Fraternity the forgotten value', *Higher Education Quarterly*, 32: 2, pp. 131–256.

28 There is plenty of room for confusion with the loose term 'community' being used in different ways with reference to schools and schooling. Some working definitions which apply within this text: 'the school community' – the people who live and work together for 195 working days each year within a particular school – staff, pupils and parents; 'the wider school community' – the varied communities (geographical, religious, partnership, professional, governance) associated with a particular school.

29 Macmurray, J. (2012) 'Learning to be Human: the Moray House Lecture of 1958', *Oxford Review of Education*, 38:6, pp. 661–674.

30 McLean, A. (2004) *The Motivated School*, London: Sage.

31 Dweck, C. (2006) *Mindset: How You Can Fulfil Your Potential*, New York: Random House.

32 Fielding, M. (2013) 'Still learning to be human', lecture delivered at Moray House School of Education, 2.5.13.

33 Murphy, D. (2013) *Professional School Leadership: Dealing with Dilemmas,* Edinburgh: Dunedin Academic Press (2nd edition).

34 Weick, K. (1976) 'Educational organizations as loosely coupled systems', *Administrative Science Quarterly*, 21:1, 1–19.

35 Audit Scotland (2014) *School Education* @ http://www.audit-scotland.gov.uk/docs/local/2014/nr_140619_school_education.pdf, accessed 13.08.14.

36 Recently a small number of authorities have begun to experiment with running some services jointly.

37 Reform Scotland (2013) *By Diverse Means p.5,* @ http://reformscotland.com/public/publications/bydiversemeans1.pdf .

38 Sahlberg, P. (2011) 'Lessons from Finland' in *American Educator,* Summer 2011.

39 A standard expression of the 'liberal education curriculum' is that it gives access to the 'best that has been thought and said'. My addition of 'done' is intended to emphasise the importance of practical action.

40 This section is mainly concerned with headteachers, but all those in leadership roles in a school are 'school leaders' and share in the 'headship' of the school.

41 Gronn, P. (2003) *The New Work of Educational Leaders.* London: Paul Chapman Publishing, pp. 147ff.

42 MacBeath, J. et al (2009) *The recruitment and retention of Headteachers in Scotland* @ http://www.scotland.gov.uk/Publications/2009/11/05105339/0, p54, accessed 13.08.14.

43 OECD (2007) *Quality and Equity in Scottish Schooling* Paris: OECD, pp. 32–33.

44 Meyer, H., *Reforming Social Democracy: the good society project*, available at http://www.social-europe.eu/occasional-papers/op-4-reforming-social-democracy-good-society-project/, accessed 25.08.14

45 Scottish Government (2014), *Education Working For All! Commission for Developing Scotland's Young Workforce Final Report*, available at http://www.scotland.gov.uk/ Publications/2014/06/4089, accessed 25.08.14

Extracts from pre-publication reviews of 'Schooling Scotland'

Full copies of all the reviews can be found online on the book's homepage at
http://www.postcardsfromscotland.co.uk/book_07.html

Daniel Murphy can pick his way through educational policy, but he also knows schools . . . this clarion call for rethinking an education system that has "reached its limit" . . . is accompanied by a downloadable collection of richly detailed observations from an education road trip. The industrious, eclectic thrum of 21st-century schools is palpable . . . [in] vivid, jargon-free prose.

Henry Hepburn, senior reporter,
Times Educational Supplement Scotland

This is a short but surprisingly full book enhanced . . . by an on-line source of case study accounts which adds significant colour . . . a must read for every adult in Scotland . . . Well read and researched, he uses his extensive experience to lay out his case. It is very persuasive . . . It is writing full of optimism as all good postcards ought to be.

Ken Cunningham, General Secretary,
School Leaders Scotland

. . . the author's passion for education, for schooling but most of all for children shone through on every page . . . he reminds us all about the primary purpose of school education: to teach young people how to live in community.

Eileen Prior, Executive Director,
Scottish Teacher Parent Council

Schooling Scotland *is an energising, uplifting read. It makes clear, good sense of the policies and attitudes that influence (and sometimes limit) current school practice in Scotland . . . a most readable, interesting text that captures for the non-specialist what it is like currently in Scotland's schools – exciting, interesting, challenging . . . the schooling of the future is redefined and a clear way forward identified.*

Jackie Dunlop, Depute Headteacher

Book Series from Argyll Publishing and the Centre for Confidence and Wellbeing

This series of short books is designed to stimulate and communicate new thinking and ways of living. The first volumes appeared in late 2012 priced £5.99 to £7.99.

Series editor and advisory group: Carol Craig of the Centre for Confidence and Wellbeing is the series editor. She is supported by a small advisory group comprising Fre Shedden, Chair of the Centre's Board, Professor Phil Hanlo and Jean Urquhart MSP.

Also published as e-books